Failure to Launch
How to Get Your Teens and Young Adults to Independence

Ellen Gibran-Hesse

Launch Press Publications ⅋ Belmont, California, U.S.A.

Failure to Launch: How to Get Your Teens and Young Adults to Independence

Copyright 2009 Ellen Gibran-Hesse

All rights reserved. No part of this book may be reproduced or transmitted in any form or by any means, electronic or mechanical, including photocopying, recording or by any information storage and retrieval system, without written permission from the authors, except for the inclusion of brief quotations in a review.

Launch Press Publications
PO Box 267
Belmont, CA 94002-0267

This book is intended to provide accurate information. However, in a time of rapid change, it is difficult to ensure that all information provided is entirely accurate and up to date. Therefore, the author and the publisher accept no responsibility for any inaccuracies or omissions and specifically disclaim any liability, loss, or risk, personal or otherwise, which is incurred as a consequence, directly or indirectly, of the use and/or application of any of the contents of this book.

ISBN: 978-0-9819138-0-3

Failure to Launch: How to Get Your Teens and Young Adults to Independence

Table of Contents

Introduction v
How to Use This Book vi
Chapter 1 What Went Wrong 1
Chapter 2 Justin, A Success Story 7
Chapter 3 What is Our Job as Parents To Young Adults? 17
Chapter 4 Preparing the Ground for the Garden 21
    Encouragement 21
    Anger Management 24
Chapter 5 Planting the Seeds of Success 31
    Dreams, Visualizations, and Self-fulfilling Prophecies 31
    Create a Willing Spirit 33
    Plan B 37
    S.A.G.E. Parenting 40
Chapter 6 Great Expectations 45
    Sleep No More 46
    Judgment Center Construction 47
    Going with the Process 48
Chapter 7 Deal Breakers 51
    Drugs and Other Addictions 51
    Abuse and Abusive Relationships 62
Chapter 8 Boundaries and Bubbles 67
    Boundaries and Our Need to Protect 67
    Bubbles and Goose Bumps 73
Chapter 9 Tools For Knowing Your Young Adult 77
    Visuals, Auditories, and Kinesthetics 77
    Humans Needs Psychology 81
    Finding a Language of Loving Support 86
Chapter 10 Skills My Teen Needs to Have 89
    The Basics List 89
Chapter 11 Rut Thinkers and the College Fairy 111
Chapter 12 If Not College, Then What? 117
    The College Track Toward Employment 118
    Jobs and Technical Schools 125
Conclusion 129

Author's Note

All of the people in my book are real and the incidents are real and told from my perspective. I have changed the names and identities to protect the privacy of the people involved but they have my deepest gratitude for sharing their trials and challenges. While it is easy to judge others and their mistakes, the fact is we all have made these mistakes and worse. Even when they appear to be very wrong, I never have doubted that these were people who loved each other. Often, a tool that will work in parenting one child may fail dismally with another. We don't often see that it is the tool and not the child who is to blame. In the words of Tina Nocera of ParentalWisdom.com, "Kids don't come with manuals." My hope is that this will at least help.

Introduction

I have been raising *kids* in some capacity since I was a child. I was the oldest of seven children, all born within eight years. My earliest memory is of handing my mother a cloth diaper for her to change one of my two little brothers, Wee One, or George Jr., and Bill. I was about two or three years old. As a baby boomer and in an era before birth control, putting the oldest daughter to work as a nanny or babysitter was not uncommon and perhaps remains common today in other countries with larger families. However, the task of maid and nanny in my family sent me running for college at age 18.

Attending college was uncommon for a girl in a blue-collar family, but I found the resources myself. Since age 14, I had tried to commit suicide and was severely depressed by the overwhelming adult burdens, as well as being an honor student, and I needed to break free. Stories such as mine weren't unique. For many centuries, having children was not a real choice. They were a consequence of sex and they came unbidden. They were at least useful in their ability to work and later take care of elderly parents. Many people in my age group tell me of needing to get away from dysfunctional families that were driving them to suicide, depression, alcoholism, low self-esteem, and a variety of rebellious or self destructive behaviors. It is with shock that we watch over 22 million adult children (according to the census bureau) return home from college or failed jobs to continue living as *children*.

I earned a Bachelor of Science in psychology, which is not surprising since I had been reading Sigmund Freud in my teen years to self heal from my depressions. I was also working as a nurse's aide to get through college, and upon getting my degree and finding it unemployable, I continued in nursing and became a hemodialysis technician, which meant putting patients on kidney dialysis machines. I took a turn into law and became a lawyer after ten years in nursing, and worked as a lawyer part-time for over 12 years as I raised my two sons, who are now 19 and 22. All along the way, my gift has been one of support and advocacy. I've run numerous volunteer organizations, including a teen skate park, an elementary school lunch program, a lunch program to feed the homeless at a local charity organization, tutoring students in reading at the elementary school level, and mentoring young girls and women.

The bottom line has been a lot of self-education and training in coaching young adults, teens, and their parents on how to negotiate the rocky road to independence. It actually can be quite smooth and enjoyable and that is my goal in helping others. I have picked up numerous tools and insights along the way that I have culled into a doable program. What is surprising is that no comprehensive program yet exists, but the tools are lying around like autumn leaves, fresh for the raking. These programs and tools that I have picked up have cured me of my depressions and helped me to get others out of the same sorts of fogs and on the road to success, however they wish to define it. And that, my friend, is tool number one. It is the individual who defines what success is. Once you find that, the rest is easy. So let's go on down the road like Dorothy to Oz and break this down.

How to Use This Book

With most *how to* books, there seems to be two ways to read them and use them. You can read them all the way through like instruction manuals or you can skip to the parts you want and read other areas as time and your interest permit. I'm trying to address both ways. Some people want to breath it all in, to understand all of it like a well worn map. Others just want what will get them through the problem. There are some urban myths out there that need to be re-examined. How we behave is mostly determined by the assumptions we make. Often we believe that our assumptions are the one and only truth and we stop looking at what they are and if they may be wrong. One common assumption is that today's young adults are so spoiled that they don't want to take the risk to go out and try to re-create their at-home lifestyle. If I hear one more time that it is *too expensive out there*, I'm going to scream. It is always too expensive out there. Learning how to position yourself for life and success is part of growing up. Secondly, *kids* aren't simply spoiled and lazy. By and large, they are totally unprepared to be anything other than students. They lack necessary life skills that we adults have long ago assumed came naturally.

I will give some history we have lived but of which we don't understand the impact. Part of the problem is that parenting styles have changed within the last 50 years, as well as the construct of the family dynamics. The biggest focus of my book is that we shouldn't be changing the young adult as much as changing the parental input and style. This is more a crisis of leadership and mentoring rather than defects in our young people. I realize most parents will want to skip that part and go right to launching and that is fine. Parenting can remain in need of update and relearning and still get a young adult launched. It will go quicker and have better interactions if the parenting can be adjusted to better understand the nature of young adults and how best to work with them. In his popular TV show, Dr. Phil will frequently say that a particular client family needs a leader. However, most of us never got the leadership training we needed. The bottom line is that I want to provide you with that help and support. In the end it is about creating successful young adults and good parent-adult child interactions.

Chapter 1 What Went Wrong

In 2005, I was sitting in a seminar on how to launch a public speaking career. I am so lucky to live in the San Francisco Bay area, as there are so many learning opportunities and I love learning! This was a class put on by the Learning Annex, which is an adult learning company that teaches all kinds of interesting and informative classes. There are classes on investment, creating various types of businesses, how to improve your love life—anything and everything it seems—and I believe there was even one on spicing up your sex life by learning to pole dance. Experts come from all over the country or are local, and they typically teach a three-hour class. It gives them a chance to share their knowledge and for the inquisitive among us to learn about so many things. Famous people have taught at these, and they put on Wealth Expos with Donald Trump, George Forman, Tony Robbins, and many more that tour throughout the year in various cities around the country. I will list resources at the end of the book and on my website at www.kidsoutnow.com because I am big believer in letting people find out resources for self development that fits their needs and personalities.

I had just started to really get interested in creating a coaching business to reach more parents and young adults, and even though it was December, the busiest time of my year, this public speaking seminar seemed too important to pass up. Classes at the Learning Annex are usually in hotel conference rooms in downtown San Francisco and the sites get decided at the last minute depending on how many people sign up to attend. If it is a small group, a small room is booked, if it's a large group, a conference room might get booked. I love the beauty of downtown San Francisco during the holiday season, so off I went. Actually there were about 30 of us, so we got to be in a lovely room in a hotel down by Fisherman's Wharf. Our speaker was a master hypnotist and business consultant, Jim Fortin. Jim had us go around the room and tell what we wanted to speak about or what we thought we wanted to speak about. I think some people just want to speak because they love the spotlight. Most of us wanted to share our knowledge, wit, or wisdom with a larger audience and public speaking gives us that opportunity. I think I was one of three that wanted to work with teens or young adults. But the other two, coming from backgrounds in social work that focused on teens out of control, were more interested in tips on controlling behavior, whereas my focus is on developing successful young adults and better family relationships. Most mental health professionals see bad behavior in a dependent child as something that needs fixing in the child. But for those of you who have seen the TV show *Nanny 911* or the National Geographic channel show *The Dog Whisperer,* much of the behavior of our dependents, whether they are children or dogs, is a result of the failure in leadership that we as parents need to present. If we change, the dynamics change. We are currently in a parenting mindset that isn't working and the need to change that mindset is growing every year.

The analogy I use is from a not so distant history. It is hard for us to believe now, but there was a very long time in history when everyone accepted that the world was flat and if you sailed off to the horizon, you risked falling off the edge. We can laugh at such a mindset because we have a different mindset. Plenty of proof abounded even then that the world wasn't flat. The moon, the sun, and the planets all appear fairly round. However, if you have that mindset, you say it is a flat disk. Perception is everything. The world is not flat. We see it differently and it has led us to grand new adventures.

Another way I explain it is that what we are going to do as parents is analogous to building a house. You need a certain number of tools to do the job right. You could use a stone instead of a hammer to pound in the nails if you were a caveman and had nothing else. You could use a knife instead of a saw if you were so limited. The house would get built. It might have lot of problems and not look as nice but it would still be a house. I'm here to tell you that the good tools are around us, and I'll teach you how and when to use them. You will have to refine their use and maybe find new tools and uses. A house and a family are always changing, needing little repairs, needing new rooms, redoing old rooms, and so forth. Control alone is like saying the house is going to stay just the same year in and year out. I don't know about your house, but in the last few years I have needed a new roof, the landscape dies and needs to be replaced, the fire detectors got old and I needed new ones, and the furnace needs things that I can't even comprehend sometimes! You get the picture.

Back to my speakers' class. This one guy, Tom, who worked with troubled teens confidently, announced that he was going to help you "tame your teen!" Yep, he knew how to do it. And I'll be honest; he may know how to do it. I haven't taken his class and he seemed like a nice and personable guy. He might work just fine for some parents and some families. But during the break he came over to me and asked me why this phenomenon of young adults returning home to live is happening. The last statistic I heard from the census bureau was that 22 million young adults in this country alone are still living at home with their parents. That means that the siblings and teens behind them will be boosting that number upward. I have also heard that one third of 18- to 34-year-olds are living at home with one of their parents. Magazines and news articles report it as a worldwide epidemic. Some cultures prefer that young adults live at home till they are married but there is a huge difference between those that live at home because they are not prepared to be on their own and those that live at home because it is real choice and they contribute to the family. We are talking here about young adults who frequently are returning from college and remaining without a job or appear to be without any adult goals or skill sets. It is as if they suddenly lost their way after high school without a snowball's chance in Hades of finding it. And parents are then in shock. I love that look of lost parents. It is almost the same as their adult children! This is Dr. Phil's number one written request to his TV show. I love Dr. Phil but I think he is pretty lost on getting these people help himself. He always ends by sending the *mooching* child off with some job counselor and giving the *spineless* parent a little kick in the seat to stop tolerating such irresponsible behavior, case closed. Then a week or two later, the same situation shows up.

Tom of "tame your teen" was asking me in utmost seriousness because he had a 21-year-old son sitting at home, lost! But it did get me thinking about some of the root causes. Many aspects of parenting have changed since my parents had me and my

Chapter 1 What Went Wrong

siblings. Many aspects of our society have dramatically changed since then. Two huge changes in the family have been that the survival rate of children and parents has improved very much. My father's father died of tuberculosis along with one or two of his adult brothers. My grandmother, Neva, was left to raise ten and eight year-old girls and a six year-old son who was my father. The little brother after me, Wee One as my parents called him, died three months after he was born from a rare skin condition that caused him painful boils. The condition today is not fatal if treated with steroids. Without vaccines, antibiotics, and our safety conscious society, children and parents died before their time. Added to that is the advent of birth control and legal termination of pregnancies which happened in the 1960's. No longer being at the mercy of having unplanned children changed lives forever. Families can now be planned according to energies and resources. Although my mother said she had tried spermicidal foams and condoms, something clearly did not work as she had seven children in eight years. She said that birth control failed. In my human sexuality class at the University of Washington, we learned that a formula of the age of the woman times the number of children had to equal some number before the obstetrician could tie a woman's reproductive tubes in the decades that my mother was having children. In short, having many children was still preferred. My mother, at age 35 with six living children, qualified, and she accepted the doctor's offer to "tie her tubes." Today we cannot fathom someone else deciding if our family size is socially acceptable. Those were different times. As I tell my sons, they are a new generation of children who are truly wanted. They are planned for and cherished for the most part. Not all children are so lucky, but the choice is now there and it is more common than not. For my parents' generation, birth control wasn't much of an option; children showed up as they had done for centuries and you did the best you could with them. In an agrarian society and in many developing countries, a lot of children meant a lot of free labor. My parents made it pretty clear, to me at least, that they would not have had so many children. I was made to understand that for the most part I was not wanted. But they took great pride in caring for us nonetheless. A roof over our heads, food in our mouths, and clothes on our back were a mark of parenting success.

Children were expected to follow the rules of the parents and authorities in the world around us because otherwise we would literally be hit, slapped, and punished. The duty of children was also to bring no shame to the parents and to bring admiration by behaving and "turning out well." In no way was there real consideration for the person inside, the personality, or that emotional needs of children were as important as physical needs. Survival and a socially acceptable image were the only things needed to present as a good parent and a good offspring. This has been the goal of families and parenting for centuries in most cultures around the globe.

Ours is a generation that plans our families to work with our careers, or at least we have that ability. We no longer find it mentally healthy to beat our kids. Perhaps with many children in the past, with such a dangerous world in terms of health and safety, it was expedient. Like a well-run military academy, you want quick compliance and a quick slap, punch, or beating got the ready compliance. We'll discuss discipline later, but keep in mind that today's children are not as fearful or beaten down as children of previous generations frequently were. I and many of my friends couldn't wait to leave home. It was a prison and at times out of our control, a hell. And that was accepted as normal. Our parents fled harsh and critical families as did their parents. That was the nature of getting on your feet. There is a saying among many now that our kids are too soft; they don't have the motivation to leave like they should. I believe they don't have the confidence or tools to leave and that is easily fixed.

Another excuse given for young adults staying at home is that they are over-protected. With fewer children there is an intensive investment of resources and, as with anything, if you have only one of or two of an item, you are perhaps a bit over-protective and tend to cherish it. If something happens to that cherished item, all your time, effort, and emotional investment is gone. Some of that is true. We have become over-protective.

When I was about three, I was freely wandering around my block. Think of that for a moment. We children ran free in the neighborhood. Mothers sent you out to play and you stayed out until it was time to come in and eat or go to bed or had to take a bathroom break. Babysitters were for at night when you were home in bed and the parents went out for an evening. One evening when I was about three, a little neighbor girl decided to take me to her grandmother's house several blocks away to visit. I was dubious even at three years old because the rule was to stay on my block, but she was older and talked me into it. I remembered train tracks and it seemed like a long way away as I had no idea where I was in relation to home. I got there and was playing with other children when the grandmother told my friend to take me home. She had heard on the radio that a little girl had gone missing in our area and she feared it might be me! It was! I remember being lifted onto my father's shoulders to view a neighborhood crowd, some tearful, all happy and relieved. I would discover years later that The Lindberg kidnapping haunted so many of them during that time. Charles Lindberg had been a famous aviator who had been the first to fly across the Atlantic. He was a star and hero in his day. He married and his baby was kidnapped. It was the news of the day as everyone waited for the child's return. How could anything so horrible happen to one so golden? The child was found dead and the fear of stranger abductions ran rampant as the nation shared in the grief of this horrible tragedy with that family. We make efforts to keep our children, our precious emotional treasures, safe, and one fear that we cannot prepare for adequately is that some stranger will take our child and torture and kill him or her. As with many fears, the anxiety drives us to over-compensate. My children never went around the block without me. Well, until they were older that is. And even then there would be the occasional alert of someone stopping children walking home from the middle school only three blocks away. Then mothers would swarm the area like angry fire ants looking for any suspicious characters.

That over-protective attitude seeped into other areas. As my insurance agent said, he could go to all sorts of places as a kid and it helped to develop a sense of confidence as he made decisions and ran his social life and met social challenges. Now his daughter must wait in the Catholic school parking lot for him to get her and all of her activities are planned and monitored. In place of going outside to play, we parents became compelled to find activities and social situations such as play dates and all sorts of extra-curricular activities. Perhaps, we unwittingly became too involved and took away a sense of exploration and confidence in doing things on one's own at an early age. We become leaders in those activities and competitive as to how our kids are doing and measuring up. While sportsmanship used to be valued over winning, the opportunity was never missed to promote the child's scholarly, social, or sports accomplishments. In a sad sense, I have seen too many parents lose track of who their child is in an

Chapter 1 What Went Wrong

effort to move them forward in scholarly or social standing. It is the new standard of parental success. Unfortunately, the child has become something of a product. Their hope of love is conditioned on their successes and on avoidance of their failures. Parents turn a blind eye to the cheating and stress that comes from pushing too hard. Unless teens start to develop a sense of who they are and learn that love is for that person in them—warts and all—they turn out codependent and prefer to be accommodating, and have no sense of adventure or growth. It is little wonder that when the push to perform stops, young adults come home lost. Where is the next goal, where is the next order, and who is giving it? They were never trained for leadership; they were trained to obey and perform. Some parents will say that their children hold leadership abilities in school, and that is good. However, leadership in running your life, making your own choices, and handling your own responsibilities is missing for the most part. Responsibility has to be more than making good grades or doing well on the numerous and ridiculous numbers of tests. It is being the one in charge, making the decisions, and accepting the success and failure on your own. Our young adults have never been in that position and are unprepared on graduation day to accept it in almost any form.

I am an animal lover. I just find them wonderful, whether they are wild or domesticated. I discovered Cesar Milan of the National Geographic channel show, *The Dog Whisperer* and was enthralled by his use of dog psychology. Cesar grew up on a farm in Mexico and has a gift for "rehabilitating dogs, training people." He comes into a situation and usually the dog owner has a story or excuse for the unwanted behavior. Cesar educates them that it isn't the excuse; it is the way they are reacting to the dog and to the behavior. Now I don't want to compare your precious child to a dog, but we are animals even if we are human beings. He then educates them to become the *pack leader*. As with the situation of our having few children and wanted children, people are very invested emotionally and otherwise in their dogs. He teaches the dog owner to become a "calm and assertive energy." With a few other tools, he has them in control of the situation. It is the situation that gets controlled, not the dog. It isn't the dog as much as the owner who has to learn to master handling situations that can trigger unwanted behavior. The whole idea of calm and assertive leadership is what we want, whether handling dogs or handling children or situations. Our generation is much more patient when our kids are little, but we lose it around the teen years. I really try to get my parents to find it again. No one responds well to out of control yelling and put-downs. Calm, assertive leadership, putting your teen and young adult into responsible situations and helping them learn to handle them is the key to developing independence and a good parent-adult child relationship.

We as parents start to abrogate our role as a parent, as a *family leader* as Dr. Phil says, pretty much around the time our children go off to middle school. If the family has had a stay at home parent, who is usually the mother, she will start to find a part-time job. From here on in, the children pull away naturally to start developing friendships and social lives that are unseen and uncontrolled by the parents. For most of us, it has been cultural wisdom that our job at this point is to control in military fashion their education to prepare them for college. We aren't doing things as a family as much during these years. We aren't vacationing as a family; we aren't even sitting down to dinner as family. Mother doesn't have time to cook, so fast food is readily available, and even prepared foods are found in the local super market. Studies have been done that kids in middle school and on up want more parent participation in their lives and for some reason, we are already off doing our own thing, thinking that if we help them get their driver's license, they will be free and so will we. Of course, they must appear to be following our rules on certain things but mainly they are ready to launch into college and we feel our job is pretty much done. Or so conventional wisdom would have us believe. This is the biggest lie we face. It is, *if they go to college they will get a good job.* We are going to explore how college has never been about getting a job. That is an *earth is flat* myth. And no matter how many statistics are coming our way, we prefer to believe the myth because it is the only game in town that we know about in terms of parenting. We are going to look at how to re-engage and have an enjoyable leadership role in our children's' lives that moves them to whatever they need to establish a career. In short, we are going to look at becoming "calm and assertive leaders" and actually loving the family we have created. ✍

Chapter 2 Justin, A Success Story

What started me coaching others grew out of a disaster. I was divorced after 18 years of marriage and suddenly a single mom of a 13-year-old and 10-year-old. Although I was a lawyer, most of my time had been as a stay at home mom with enough law practice to stay current. I felt too rusty for a full time job in a law firm and returned to school to get my Master's in law in intellectual property. Intellectual property is the area of law that encompasses patents, trademarks, and copyright, all much needed if I was to continue my pursuit of being an entertainment law attorney. I finished my degree in 2003, ready for my movie star client list. Alas, being in the San Francisco bay area, the competition was intense. I went to work part-time in 2004 for a good friend who had her own bankruptcy law practice while I looked for full time work. It seemed like the ideal situation. I liked going to court and learning another area of law to add to my expertise, and she needed help with the practice.

But all was not well for my friend, Sara. Her husband, Art, was suffering from some sort of illness and the workload at their law office where he was a partner was piling up while Art went through various tests. It didn't help that Sara's nephew had come to live with them from the Midwest the previous summer. Art had never liked the time and attention that Sara gave to Justin. Although Art had three children from a previous marriage that stayed with them on occasion, he seemed to be one of those people who wanted family life to be just the two of them. I wondered later as Sara told me that she thought his problems could be anxiety attacks or severe allergies if the problem wasn't having Justin in his home for eight months. I liked Art but he ignored me in the office and I could hear him complain bitterly about Justin to Sara. He was indignant and demanding that Sara do something about Justin, who had sloppy habits and left milk out and didn't put things away. Since he had children in Justin's age range of 19, I was a little surprised that he just didn't talk man to man to Justin and remind him to put things away. But there clearly was an expectation that Justin was Sara's problem and Art was very unhappy.

Sara seemed lost. A loving and caring person, she was like so many of us from a generation of parents who thought the best way to get compliance from a child or teen was harsh criticism. The fact that harsh criticism frequently becomes emotional and verbal abuse remains unacknowledged by and large in the mental health field even today. Sara complained that Justin was clinging; he hadn't made friends to hang out with, didn't have his driver's license, and only worked part-time when he needed full-time work with benefits. His learning disabilities and difficulty spelling were alarming. In Sara's mind, if Justin was to succeed, he had to go to college as she had. That's the myth, right? Go to college if you want a good job. In all those eight months, all she had been able to do was attempt to correct his academic short-comings by having him read books, write journals, and do book reports. To her thinking, he read well and comprehended well, therefore the problem was just a lack of spelling and writing practice. If he had those he would succeed in college and of course get a good job. How many times have we heard this refrain? It is a lie. I want you to start to understand that. Does it happen ever? Yes. People win the lottery too, but I'm not spending a ton of money on that one.

Eager to please, Justin complied. But no matter how hard he tried, Art was dissatisfied and ever more upset. The home environment had become a powder keg and then, in April the explosion hit. Sara called me to ask if Justin could come spend the weekend with me until Art calmed down. While reading on the sofa with Justin, she was shocked when Art, sitting in a chair nearby reading his newspaper, flung it down and stormed out of the house. I asked if he had commented or complained or if there had been an angry exchange. Nothing. He just blew up without saying much. I said of course Justin could come spend the weekend. When Sara and Justin arrived, they both looked shell shocked. The explosion had baffled them both. They had obviously done something wrong, but what was it? They were at a loss. Sara called me later and said that Art was still on the rampage and perhaps since he was so upset, I shouldn't return to work for a while. Then I was shell-shocked. I was a single mom. I was living off child support and the equity line on my very large house. This was a third mouth to feed and his part-time job was over half an hour away by train. In fact, the commute was more like an hour away if you added in time to and from the train station. Since he didn't drive, I was the shuttle to the train station. I was overwhelmed.

As a little background to Justin's life and our relationship, let me explain a few things. Sara and I were in law school together when her younger half-sister, Helen, got pregnant. Helen was only 16 and their mother was a blind piano bar entertainer with a drinking problem. She worked at night and slept during the day. Helen's pregnancy was a surprise. There were suspicions that Helen preferred partying to school, and once she had Justin, she dropped out of school and never got her GED. Good people at heart, both Helen and her mother had trouble with alcohol use and this impacted their ability to parent. Helen didn't work; she lived with her mother or with friends. She was a wild child. Instead of putting him up for adoption, she kept little Justin. As expected, grandmother came to the rescue and raised Justin until he was about six. Justin remembered his father for a short while in his life around three years old and the physical abuse of his father pushing him down the stairs and hitting him. Father disappeared after a short time, much to Justin's relief. He resurfaced when Justin graduated from high school to apologize for being a poor father and to show off his new life of a home, cars, boat, wife, and two sons. He gave Justin money for his graduation and said, "keep in touch." In commenting to Justin about how much he loved his sons, no mention was made that Justin was just as loved or even cared about. Justin never looked back.

Meanwhile, Helen married, and at age 10, Justin welcomed a new half-sister. At age 15, a second sister came along. But life was far from idyllic. Mother drank heavily. Justin changed diapers and fed the baby, himself, and his other sister. His stepfather was very critical and judgmental and the two clashed. Verbal fights were common as were threats and hitting things. As Justin struggled with learning disabilities and school, he worked part-time at a Wal-Mart type store, learning retail and doing well. His money was frequently *borrowed* by mom for cigarettes, diapers, and beer. When she was sober, he remembered the house looking nice, dinners that were good, and

Chapter 2 Justin, A Success Story

his mother's fun spirit. But those memories were overshadowed by frequent moves, new schools, and more upheavals.

Aunt Sara had taken to bringing him out to California for summer vacations when he was about eight years old. She worried over his time spent in front of the TV lost in a world of his imagination to escape the chaos of his life. However, since she had her law practice, she needed time to catch up so I would invite him to our house for a weekend or outing. He became like a cousin to my sons. In his last year of high school, his stepfather left his mother. The two girls were taken to their father's parents while the legal battle began. Helen had no income and went to live with her mother. But Aunt Sara set Justin up in his own apartment as he was 18 and starting his senior year. Continuing to work, living on his own so that he could stay with the same school and teachers that had helped him so much, Justin found that life on his own could be overwhelming. At times, he didn't think he had the strength to continue. Thanks to his teachers and his own determination, he survived and graduated. Worried about him, Aunt Sara brought him out to live with her until he could get on his feet. After eight months, it hadn't happened and now Justin was abandoned again at my house, no further ahead than when he came out here.

It took me about a week to realize I was in a worst-case scenario. Art was still thundering mad over Justin's mere existence. Sara was beginning to doubt that she had a viable marriage and Justin was eating up his small savings to travel to his part-time job. Sara began to tell me that if Justin wasn't moving forward then I should just throw him out. Helen was calling drunk at all hours to complain that I thought I knew her son, but I knew nothing! Great. She resented that I had written an angry note to Sara saying this was an unfair burden. For some odd reason, the whole family had decided that if I lived in a big house, I could afford to take care of one more child. It felt like I was dealing with an insane asylum. I realized that I had to break off contact with all that dysfunction and just focus on Justin. In the meantime, however, I had my own sons to care for. This was not going to be easy.

Once I got methodical about it, it wasn't that hard. Justin seemed to me to be a haunted and terrified young man. He would say or do whatever you wanted to hear to get along. Sara used to complain that he lied but I felt he did it out of defense. He just wanted to be left alone and not judged or hurt. We are usually so critical of our teens, assuming they are young adults bent on trying to be inconsiderate of us and all we do. Usually, they just don't have the ability yet to multi-task and organize. Our expectations are wrong and research is backing up the fact that our assumptions are wrong. The young adult brain is undergoing huge changes that make adult behavior on a consistent basis impossible. I have great patience and I needed it then. Justin had a tendency to cling to me. It felt to me like when a toddler doesn't even let you talk on the phone. It felt suffocating, but then, I have always been pretty self-sufficient whether or not I wanted to be. I realized that he probably was frightened moving out here and he had no one in his family to depend on. Since his grandmother was blind, I suspected that he had kept close to her both for her sake and his. Pushing him away would probably panic him. So I decided to turn his constant presence into hands-on tutoring. I could use it to motivate him, teach him, and model adult behavior for him.

On many different fronts, we had to build up his self esteem, get his driver's license, get him a car, get him a full-time job, get him to explore social opportunities, and get him moved into his own place. This was the game plan. Each day one or most of those lessons were in play. He had to learn to build up healthy boundaries with his family. They had lots of demands on him; he had to start to decide what he wanted. Mother's drunken rants could be stopped with a polite comment such as "I'll talk to you when you are sober" and then hanging up and not answering her repeated attempts to call back and swear. He had catered to her drama and upsets for so long and they were emotionally draining. It had never occurred to him that he was entitled to set limits as to how he would be treated. In the Jerry Springer world he grew up in, you had to be verbally nasty, cutting, and even cruel to get others to back off. He was a kind-hearted person and that nasty, cruel attitude wasn't what he wanted. Aunt Sara was furious. Although we talked for the first few months, Sara's husband didn't calm down for five weeks after the initial blow up. She had to pretend she had broken off all contact with him and then sneak around to see him. I was fast realizing that, in his family, no one was willing to help me. Only his grandmother appreciated what I was doing for her cherished grandson. But the others now expected me to care for Justin and follow their demands of how to raise him as if I were merely their nanny and servant. It left me not talking to any of them anymore. They were livid. How dare I?! I was terrified by all the responsibility left at my door but I had faith that it would work out. I had to stay focused on making it happen in a healthy way for all of us. Remember, I still had my own sons to raise. At this point, my oldest was graduating high school and my youngest was 15, just beginning high school.

One thing I needed as top priority was getting Justin to decide where he wanted to go career-wise. The company he worked for had promised him full employment and now, eight months later, it looked no more real than when he started. We discussed how this was the trend. Part-time work was cheaper in retail since they didn't have to pay benefits. Basically, in Justin, they had a good worker who had worked retail throughout high school. He was cheerful and willing to come in whenever they needed. As long as they didn't make the hours full-time, it worked well for them. It worked to a point for Justin too, as this was the only security he had. He had friends; he was earning something. We talked a lot about his interests, work he would like to do, and aspects of work he liked. We looked into his starting his own pet-sitting business. He learned to make his own business cards, which we took around to vets and pet stores. Not having a car made this impractical, however. It was hard to do dog walking and pet-sitting when you only had public transportation and I couldn't take the time to chauffeur him everywhere. Also, establishing any business requires a lot work to build up a clientele. With that realization, he put that dream back on the shelf.

He loved to travel so we went to the airport and looked over jobs posted on the bulletin board there. In all of this I was holding his hand through learning to investigate and research interests and pair them with potential job fields. In career tech education, this is called "exploring career pathways." Initially, Justin worried that he would have to take any job offered. I had to convince him that is was all exploration. If he found out that it wasn't what he wanted, he thanked them and moved on. He got an interview for one job that sounded interesting and interviewing was his strong suit. He decided against it although they were willing to hire him. The hours were irregular and not full-time as he wanted. It empowered him to see that he could refuse the employer; he wasn't just a victim to be rejected by the boss. In all of these, we had job specific resumes so he was learning to build upon the skills he had, and once it was on paper, he realized he did have skills. The lack of driving was creating a big problem. It also

Chapter 2 Justin, A Success Story

impacted his self-esteem. When teens younger than him were off driving, he was confined. Young adults look very much to their peers to see if they measure up, and the lack of a skill such as driving implies a failure to make it to the next level of adulthood.

Thus began the journey to driving. This was concurrent with job hunting and resume skill building, and learning to put his family relations on healthier footing. Every day was an involved journey of self-growth and movement towards higher levels of maturity. Driving was a unique problem. In the past his mother would take him to bars where she was a regular. He was able to get in and even was served liquor after hours because of her standing with the establishments. She not only wanted a drinking buddy, she also wanted someone to drive her home. But no one had taught him. His stepfather had tried and after jerking the wheel while Justin was driving and nearly creating an accident, Justin refused further lessons with him. His grandfather had tried and gave up after a few attempts. Still, his mother would pass out in the back seat after a night at the bar and have him drive her home as best he could. That ended when he was pulled over on the highway by the police for going so slow. When the officer saw the mother passed out, he had Justin follow him homeward as his escort. These were not auspicious beginnings in learning to drive.

After two tries at the written exam and failing both times, I put Justin on the computer tests offered by the Department of Motor Vehicles. He did well. Off we went and he subsequently failed a third time. He was discouraged. I had done tutoring of elementary school children for reading and I felt I could figure out what went wrong and get him pointed in the right direction. I have had the ability to intuit what is going on inside the student and I hoped that gift would help here. I know he understood the material as I had tested him verbally. I knew his long term and short-term memory of the subject matter were good. As I looked over the test, I realized he missed several questions that we had gone over before the test. When I asked him about it, he admitted he did know the answers. Had he misread the question? The more we talked, the quicker I realized he had test anxiety. When I asked him if this was possible, he admitted that test anxiety haunted him all through school. "Well, this is good news! We can cure this!" I said. He looked at me as if I had lost my mind. Justin and I are big on humor. Life, if nothing else, is a giant sitcom that must keep God rolling on the floor laughing. We might as well get in the spirit too. I told him that tests are like video games. If you do them over and over, you get to move to the next level. You need to get prepared for the next monster, the next obstacle, and pick up the lucky symbols that give you a new life or more points. It is learning the game. He knows the game; he's done it three times. Now to win, we just needed to perfect the strategy! I joked that every day off from work he had, we'd be in the D.M.V. taking the test, getting better and better. We'd get to know the people that work there so that he'd walk in the door and we'd shout out *hellos* and ask after them. It would be old home week every time we went. I wanted him to enter the building with a sense of humor, not the sense of dread and cold fear that we who have had test anxiety experience and which prepares us to fail. I wanted him to see it as a place he could enjoy because he is a people person, and not to think of it as the moment when he would once again prove he was a failure. The focus was on what he is good with, interacting with people. The test was a mindless video game. Sometimes you win, sometimes you don't. It's just a game.

Also, what I was not doing was what Aunt Sara and a lot, of parents do and that is to scold and criticize. Somehow we think that young people need that emotional whack upside the head to get motivated to do better when all it does is add to their fear and anxiety of failure. Failure means loss of love, shame, and humiliation. I try to get all of my children to see failure as an opportunity to learn to be really good at it the next time. These challenges are like a video game to get good at and win. Bring it on! I told him he would pass eventually. They do not have unlimited sets of tests. Sooner or later you'll get one you had before. It is like redoing the level in a video game. I told him if he got one that he had before, he should miss one question so that it didn't look too perfect. And sure enough, that is exactly what happened. On his next try he got one he already had taken. Since he had memorized questions and gone over them in detail he was delirious with joy. He spent more time picking out one question to miss than he probably had done taking the rest of the test! He was in control of this outcome. He had won the video game. I can't begin to tell you how excited he was. This was a huge hurdle.

In the meantime, I was driving him to and from the train station for his commutes to his part-time job. Aunt Sara was saying that if he attended community college he could come back to live with them. He didn't want to return because we couldn't trust Art not to explode again. Given that he wanted to stay in the area around me, we needed to get him transferred to a company store nearby. We found one and he liked it. The policy was to have the manager of his current store recommend a transfer to the new store. He put in his request and fireworks began. He was suddenly not doing well enough to transfer. They felt he was *too friendly* with the customers. No, they could not allow him to transfer with the problems he was having. He was discouraged. I determined that they liked him, he was a good worker, liked by customers and co-workers, and that this was a ruse so as not to let him leave. Being 19 years old, he was skeptical that people could be like that. I told him that he couldn't afford to remain part-time. One suggestion was for me to write a letter to them on my attorney letterhead letting them know that this was a grave inconvenience for me and that it was depleting his savings to commute, which it was, and asking them to reconsider the transfer. We sent the letter up the corporate ladder to their superiors. This brought an explosion from them. They blamed him, saying that he had not been clear that he really had wanted a transfer and if that was what he wanted it would be fine, but they doubted he'd even get as many hours as he was currently getting. He was frightened and angry. He was angry that they were blaming him when they had constantly put off his requests. He was frightened that he now would lose his friendships with his current coworkers for a job with less income and hours. Had he made the wrong move? I said, "We know you can't keep this up. The commute is costing too much and they have had over eight months to hire you full-time. It is best to move on and if you get less hours then look for another job, but staying put is not an option anymore." He had to agree, but the unknown looked scary. These are the moments, parents, where you have to hand hold and encourage, be the cheer-leader, infuse the moment with the positive when even you don't know if there is a positive!

Within several weeks of the transfer, he was working full-time. He had feared losing the friends he had made at the old store but he and the managers still saw each other and they came to like and respect each other. He now had money and could start to budget beyond the small amount he was giving me for room and board. He was learning to drive and we went car shopping. He learned how to research through

Chapter 2 Justin, A Success Story

Consumer Reports whether a car was reliable and what things to check for in used cars. We learned about VIN numbers and checking them through Carfax to see if the car had a suspect history, and he researched different car insurances. There were so many life skills for him to learn from banking and understanding credit cards and credit scores, to just learning to be neat and how to organize his room and life. These are things we don't realize need to be taught. As adults who already have these skills, we somehow think they just show up in our young adult's life. They have to be taught and the mistakes have to be overlooked, not driven home with angry shouts and criticisms. All new skill sets have a learning curve of mistakes made until there is a level of mastery. We need to be compassionate but firm in achieving them. Calm, assertive leadership is the key.

By the end of August, after driving for just two months, he took his driver's test. He didn't pass. My other two sons had passed the first time, but I had spent a lot of time driving with them. He didn't pass until the third time. By then, I had learned how to be a better teacher! We used each of the moments that felt like failure to find out how to better obtain success. I didn't put all the blame on him. I was the life coach. No team goes out on the field to win without good coaching. We both learned and we both eventually succeeded. Justin was developing a life strategy.

His Aunt was not happy. In her mind, he needed to be in college, and while I was away on a vacation with my sons for my oldest son's high school graduation, she took him to the local community college near her and had him tested for his learning disabilities and talked him into going to college. When I returned, he announced fearfully that he would be going to college. I asked him where was he going to live. Aunt Sara wanted him to live with her again and then to find and move in with roommates. I was a bit dumbfounded. How would he get to work now that he was working full-time? He didn't have a regular work schedule. He worked all different hours, all different days, so how would he be able to attend classes regularly? How would he have time to study now that he was working full-time, and when he was finished with college, what job would he be able to get? He had no answers. She hadn't thought of any of this. Her only role is the one most parents have, just get them to college and then they will have a good job. I told him that if he wanted to go to college, then fine let's do it! We'd find a way. But I was hearing Aunt Sara's hopes and dreams and I wanted to know if they were his hopes and dreams. He looked relieved and said he didn't want to go. What Aunt Sara didn't understand, being an excellent student all of her life, was that he was healing from years of stress and pain being in *special education* and not doing as well as his peers. For her, education was a place where she excelled. For him it was a source of failure and low self-esteem. It was too much, given all he was learning to be independent. I suggested that since he was just getting on his feet, a better approach to college was to get settled to find a social life and a reasonable work schedule and take a fun class to get his feet wet. This was someone who had test anxiety, for whom school had been a harsh and difficult experience. I very much felt that he was still healing from his parents' divorce, contact with his long absent father, moving, and being abandoned by his family. He had been through a lot. And if there is one thing I have found, it's that sometimes you just need to settle into your new identity. I pointed out that college is a great place to meet people his own age including dating partners, but maybe to take it a bit slow.

Aunt Sara never took *no* for an answer. As an attorney and a mentor, she used every trick in the book to argue to get her way. After all, it was **the way**. As I told Justin, rather than promise her he'd go next semester or make up some lie, he could say, "I'm not ready. But thanks for the help and encouragement and I'll let you know when the time is right." We were dealing with creating healthy boundaries and an adult-to-adult relationship. The idea was that when the arguments and lectures from her began, he should cut them short with "no thanks" and to be persistent and calm. It is part of learning to be an adult and not the emotional child in these situations.

We were down to the last skill set. It was finding Justin a place to live. I introduced him to college roommate boards and online places like craigslist.com and the like. Although he had his driver's license by then, he didn't have the income yet to buy the little car I had purchased for $5000 on his behalf. Our understanding was that if he could show me a reasonable payment plan, he could buy it from me. But after looking at insurance for a young man and at the prices of living on his own, he didn't think he could do it immediately. That was fine as I could use the car for my younger son and had bought it knowing that was a possibility. In all things we did, we had back up plans. There is Plan A and then Plan B and Plan C, depending on how things turn out. This too is a life skill that needs to be taught. He settled on a place within walking distance from work. It was the home of a single working mother with two sons his age who took in two boarders to supplement her income. The room was large, the townhouse nicely furnished, and the woman warm and motherly. I would have chosen one of the places with a more traditional roommate set up that we all experience in college. A setting with young adults of similar age and experiences with finances and romances would have been more attractive to me. But I thought perhaps he needed a family atmosphere that was calm and nurturing given he never really had that before. By now he also was much better at being neat. He was a much different person leaving my house six months later than when he came in my door with his Aunt Sara. It is important to note that although Sara and I never spoke again, I encouraged his connection to her and to develop a healthier relationship with respect for boundaries, by them for him and by him for them. His family was important to him and getting along with others is probably what life is about anyway. It is another skill set. To this day, that part of his life seems much more balanced with more respect. That is what we want for our families isn't it?

So to recap, in six months Justin learned how to write resumes, job hunt, start a fledgling business, decide where his interests lie, get a driver's license and learn to drive, shop for a car, deal with banking and establishing credit, get set up in his own place and create healthier family ties. A lot of this is hands on and ongoing. He knows he can bring questions to me and I will walk him through how to figure something out. I don't judge and I turn things into a game. "How can <u>we</u> get this done or figured out?" is the name of the game. I learn from him, too. None of us in this complex world have all the answers anymore. The real skill is finding out the answers we need to know. Recently he phoned to ask how to use an American Express check. "Gift card you mean?" I asked. "No, a check," he responded. I asked to see it. It looked like a traveler's check, something you don't see much anymore now that ATMs are worldwide. The amount was for $25 and there was a line to designate a merchant or payee. I explained he could use it like a traveler's check or cash it or deposit it at his bank. It had been a holiday bonus from work. When he went to the grocery store even the clerk was unfamiliar with it but the manager knew what it was and everyone

Chapter 2 Justin, A Success Story

learned something new. He has the confidence to find out what he needs to know and engage others in the process. He is no longer afraid to ask questions for fear he will be humiliated for not knowing. He knows that if he is to manage his life, he must ask questions.

He moved out three years ago. We are still very close and have traveled to Hawaii together for his birthday and then to Las Vegas for another birthday. He is ready to travel to Europe. He has changed jobs to work in a clothing store when it became obvious that he wasn't going to be moving into management any time soon at his old job and he made a promotion to visual merchandiser in the new store. When they didn't promote him to management, he found another company and is now an assistant manager. He is learning to develop his career and move up. He sees experience and continued raises in his title and compensation as the way to work up the ladder to the job of his dreams. This is something even most adults don't do. We took a community college class together for fun and he enjoyed it. His Plan A was to pass the course with a "B". His Plan B was to drop the course if it was too much and he was failing. At the very least, he will have gone to college and learned how to be successful there. He was excited and got an "A". But he decided college isn't for him. As we always say, "now you know." But even now he is wondering if maybe some sort of career college degree in the hospitality industry might be a possibility. He is still exploring his career paths. Aunt Sara has given him one of her 20- year-old cars and has paid for its upkeep. He loves driving and I think secretly she likes that he can drive to see her or meet her for lunch. It was a big leap of faith for her to let him drive on his own. He likes who he is and loves his life. He is successfully launched and well on his way to being an adult in the way we all think of adults as handling life and their responsibilities. ✍

Chapter 3 What is Our Job as Parents To Young Adults?

Perhaps the biggest confusion in all of this is that we are confused as parents of young adults as to what our job and role in their lives should be. Clearly, by the teen years, they acquire some independence by obtaining driver's licenses, going to and from school unaided, participating in sports or other extra-curricular activities on their own, and maybe working at a job. Although some parents still monitor study habits, curfews, and other time management details, by and large, the typical teen is starting to manage aspects of their lives. The key word here is *manage* and it is here that problems arise. Jim Fay, in his series of books on parenting, does a wonderful job describing types of parenting styles that may not work well. There are Helicopter parents who hover and in the extreme are over involved and over identified with their child's accomplishments. These parents in benign form appear as their teen's manager or personal assistant, waking the child and being in charge of many details that the teen should be taking on in his or her own life. In the worst cases, their over involvement has a compulsiveness that may drive their adult children away to escape the suffocating nature of their involvement. Then there is the Drill Sergeant parent who issues orders and then expects them to be followed. This again is a parent who is not letting the teen acquire skills in life management. Part of management skills involves making choices and decisions. Your choices and decisions are yours. Often one's choices are arrived at by careful determination and experience and take on the glow of being the *right* choice. Too often, many people assume their decisions must be right for everyone, especially for their teen or young adult. However, choices are just preferences about how to handle certain circumstances. Your preferences aren't necessarily the only answer. This is hard for parents who are still stuck in the mode of instructing younger children. You pass along to your young child how to arrive at what is right. At this stage of the parenting game, you have to start letting your teen, and especially your young adult, make decisions and choices and learn from the mistakes. Our job as parents is not to make sure our teens don't make mistakes. They must and they will. That is part of learning any skill set. Your job is to help them recover and proceed to fix it and be confident that they can handle it. There is also the need to let them suffer the consequences of choices that don't turn out so well. It is not to save them from consequences. Rescuing them from the natural consequences is putting you on the path of enabler of a dysfunctional child. However, there is a fine line between helping them recover from a mistake most of us make and need help with and letting them suffer a bit so that they will be less inclined to go down that road again. Sometimes we make the wrong decision to help when it should have been to let the lesson sink in.

What is our role? It is to help them in a very discreet way and to engage them in discussions about where they are going. In these teen years, they need to be developing ideas of where they want to go career-wise. It is important that they work

Failure to Launch: How to Get Your Teens and Young Adults to Independence

for pay or for experience so as to gain experience and flesh out their interests. As much as we would love them to pick a career and stay on the narrow path to it, that is unlikely. They will change several times as they try out jobs and learn what is really involved. Our job is to make sure they understand that they have to work on figuring out what life will be like after high school and after college. The nebulous, "go to college so that you can get a good job" is absolutely zero help. Half the graduating seniors in college are going back home as no jobs showed up out of the blue as they were led to believe. Considering that only half of the people who started college graduate, you get the picture of how well that is working. Don't forget that only about a third of high school students go on to college. Ours is a generation of parents who are clinging desperately to the idea of college as the goal for success. The reality is that we have been sold an idea that, if it ever had validity, no longer does. We forgot that most of us worked and built up good job skills and good resumes. Without those, college is icing on a flat plate. There is no cake.

Our job is to continue to pass responsibility to our teens and young adults. As they hold down part time jobs, they need to pay bills either for cell phones, gas, car insurance, or the purchase of their clothes. They need to manage their time. Our job is to only intervene if they are having trouble and then we need to ask how we can help, not to barge in to get it done for them. My youngest son was a very good student in high school but there seemed to be a tendency at his school to pile on the homework and projects at the end of the year. He was so stressed out he was snapping. After ascertaining that he had managed things well but was just given way too much homework, I asked how I could help him. For one thing, he needed to vent his frustration and anger about it seeming impossible to get it all done. Sometimes they need to vent just like we do. One project involved reading a book from the 1980's and giving page references to things clearly pertinent to that time period. He had a short book, about 180 pages, so I offered to do that for him as he had only read half of it. He could read my notes and decide if I was keeping within the homework frame. He still had to write the paper, but I had essentially given him a boost with the research. He didn't think I could do it in one night. I did it in several hours. I've had practice consuming huge chunks of text and casework as a lawyer. It took the pressure off of him and let him know that when I ask how I can help, I mean it. There were no lectures about time management. The teachers clearly did not recognize the load that other teachers had put on their students. Things like that happen. Again, as Dr. Phil says, "be that soft place to fall." If you see a pattern of not managing time or projects well, it is time to have talk—not a lecture but a talk—on how to improve the management style. If they know you are a kind mentor, they will bring things to you for help trouble shooting and working out solutions.

Sometimes they can't see that things aren't working well. Our expectations have to be realistic. Their brains are still developing, and they are getting a crush of pressures from learning new life or job management skills, hormones are raging, and social life is treacherous. Assume they need support and probably don't know it. Bring that same kindness to them that you brought when they were learning to read and live life in elementary school. It will create a strong bond. A few times in college, my oldest son asked me on the edge of a deadline to read and edit a paper. He wasn't feeling strong about it. There were no lectures about deadlines, either I had time or I didn't. He knew that was my boundary. It was his choice to do it so close to the deadline; these were his consequences. But haven't we all hit deadlines or come up against things that we

Chapter 3 What is Our Job as Parents to Young Adults?

could have managed better? Generally, because it was easy for me, I was able to do it for him. He knew I would not rewrite the paper to glorify my brilliance, which my own mother loved to do and which I have seen in Helicopter parents. I kept his tone, smoothed it out, and corrected grammar. I was very pleased to see how well his writing had developed and I told him so. It was never easy for him in high school.

The bottom line is we want to share in their lives not direct them or be responsible for them. This comes from playing the role of mentor, or in Jim Fay's model, the Counselor. You have got to learn to be neutral but you have to set expectations. They must work, they must cultivate a resume with experience, they must cultivate connections for future jobs, and they must take risks and start somewhere. I am amazed when I ask parents what their teen or young adult has in mind for a career or work plans and the parents have no idea. That this continues through college truly baffles me. There should be some dialogue there. There should be some interest. Of course, they aren't going to stick to such dreams, but you want them to start thinking about it and be moving toward it. College should only be Plan A. For many it isn't even that, and that is fine. Then the conversation should be about some career field of interest. They have to get to work in some form and be moving toward some goal to decide if it fits or is to be rejected. It is easiest to start these goals and dialogues in the teen years, because once they are 18, you lose a lot of their attention. If they are used to this game plan early on, it will be easier to evolve into success. ⚄

Failure to Launch: How to Get Your Teens and Young Adults to Independence

Chapter 4 Preparing the Ground for the Garden

You can get your adult child out of the house without reading this chapter. To use gardening as an analogy, you can throw seeds on all sorts of ground and, given half a chance, they will sprout. But if you want a truly remarkable garden and a bountiful harvest then you should prepare the garden for optimum growth. You remove the weeds, dig the earth to loosen it for the seed, water it, add compost or other nutrients, and then plant the seed. However, if you are in a situation that needs quick resolution and feel pushed, you can go to the quick formula. That requires only that you make a game plan, adjust your expectations to be realistic, be supportive especially in the face of mistakes or apparent defeat, and learn some anger management and good manners, which means giving respect to another's boundaries. Easy, right? It is. When Cesar Milan, the Dog Whisperer, consults with a dog owner, he starts walking with the dog to establish a relationship and give himself the role of a calm, assertive pack leader. Then he takes the owner and puts them in the same position. In short, he models for them and then they take a turn. They may make a few mistakes, but he helps them, and most of all, he encourages them! Get calm, get assertive, enjoy the process, have your game plan in place ready to adjust as needed and move forward. But for those who need a little more ground preparation, let's start with some basics.

Encouragement

In the era before the 1960's, common discipline of children included physical abuse. "Spare the rod, spoil the child." However, this left too many of us emotionally damaged. As therapy and better parenting techniques became more discussed in the media, and we saw that many notorious murderers and criminals were and have been horribly beaten and abused, we developed a more humanistic approach to parenting. Some of this was result of the growth of the psychology movement, some came from the sensitivity to others learned from the peace movement in response to the media horrors of the Vietnam war, and some of it came from a better understanding of the horrible impact of violence on the human spirit resulting in emotional wounds that sometimes never heal, as the media turned to violence as a means of selling news. As lynching, war, and spousal abuse were examined, our social psyche told us that violence, especially physical violence, is destructive long after the violent moment.

When my own children started school, I was amazed at the generous encouragement parents gave their children despite the imperfections of their attempts to master skills. I marveled that my own parents would never heap such lavish praise upon us. It was thought to create too much pride and self-absorption in a child if a parent appeared to be almost fawning in encouragement. But this was a new era. Whether it was reading, drawing, riding a bike or kicking a ball, parents were thrilled to praise and encourage

Failure to Launch: How to Get Your Teens and Young Adults to Independence

their little ones. These were our precious children and their frustrated tantrums and cries were met with soothing and encouraging words on our part. We taught our children the "magic words" like "please" and "thank you". We embraced growth in the daily learning that was evolving right before our eyes as they mastered these skills and moved on to new levels.

But by the middle school years (which were 6th grade to 8th here in our area of California but 7th to 9th in Michigan where I grew up), we had long since stopped using "please" and "thank you" with our kids and yet felt cheated that they didn't have gratitude toward us. I say "we" and "us" to include myself, but I have since grown away from these parenting errors. We did what had been modeled for us. We came from military style parenting, the children of returning WWII vets and their spouses. Our parents were the "officers" and we were the "subordinates". We followed orders. Gone was the friendly, calm parenting as our generation reverted to what we experienced growing up. We no longer used the "please" and "thank you" model, forgetting how we once gleamed with pride when our little ones used them in talking to other adults. Maybe it was because I was a newly single mom when my sons were entering middle school that I found myself thankful for my children every day. And from then on I found myself returning to the kindness of parenting from just a few years before, and using "please" when asking my middle school aged children to do something, thanking them for efforts made, and contributions given. I did it so often that I was surprised when my sons started thanking me for taking them out to dinner, for making a meal, for washing their clothes. Just encouraging them with those magic words caused them to begin to model them back to me. I pointed out to them how much it meant to me, because in some respects we are still superiors, authority figures, and very few authority figures in the real world remember to use politeness. Perhaps they should. It creates a much different atmosphere of respect and appreciation.

Justin has been promoted into management now at age 23. This has been his dream for several years. Better pay for sure, but a lot more responsibility. In his training with the coffee chain he works for, he is moved to different stores to learn the ropes over a series of weeks. It is a bit overwhelming because he is learning the menus, the overall set up of the sales and products, and the staffing work and duties. He found that learning to delegate was a big difference from being an associate at his other job where he took orders. As he was preparing to leave his store where he had his initial training, employees bemoaned his going. They had wondered out loud to him that they didn't understand why he gave them duties and said "please" and "thank you". Justin was used to being in our family where that is the daily norm and he hadn't even thought about it. It is important how we treat each other and the people we come in contact with. Those words aren't like fine china only to be used on special occasions. They are daily affirmations of the love and respect for each other and those we come into contact with. Those words are validating and affirming of others. They show kindness and respect. I always notice that once I use them with people they start to respond in kind. It made Justin realize that he wants to treat employees with respect and in the few short weeks he was at his store, it endeared him as a "boss". I have read studies about how most people on the job feel very underappreciated and resent their jobs as a result. In the volunteer programs I have run, the same is true. People will give you their all if they feel you appreciate them.

Chapter 4 Preparing the Ground for the Garden

On the day Justin told me this story, I had run into an acquaintance in the drug store. Diane had been through a difficult divorce several years ago and felt her husband had poisoned her older children against her and was now doing the same with her 13 year -old son, Matthew. The older children, now in college, had finally understood the dynamics of their dad's tirades, but Matthew did not. One of the problems was getting Matthew to do chores around the house on a consistent basis. To Diane, he had become sullen and resentful. He had demanded that she say "please" and she felt this wasn't necessary. Her feeling was that he was a young man and he should step up and do the chores without being asked, let alone being asked politely. I was dumbfounded. Why not say "please" as it is great modeling for dealing with everyone and why not expect to have to remind the boy from time to time? I have heard this idea a lot that family members don't need to be asked politely to help. If not them, then who? Matthew is going through a lot of growth and change as well as dealing with the emotional trauma of bouncing back and forth between two very different households. He has a stepmother and a stepfather now, so none of these houses are the home he knew growing up. It is that parental inability to see the opportunities to nurture and model that I think we all need to be more aware of if we are to formulate good bonds with our kids. As she told me how she shouldn't be expected to say "please" to a family member, I remembered a movie I had seen in college. It was called *Love Story* with Ryan O'Neil as wealthy Oliver and Ali McGraw as working class Jennifer. Oliver's father disinherits his son for marrying so poorly, but the couple moves forward through college. As they try for a family, Jennifer is found to be terminally ill at age 25 and dies. The most famous line from this 1970 film is "Love means never having to say you're sorry." Even at the time, I thought that was the dumbest thing I'd ever heard. Such sentiment makes no sense other than to save face for the wrong doer, who should apologize. That is the mark of taking responsibility and of caring about others. Some of our deepest wounds come from people who never acknowledged what they did or that they were remorseful. Many times, forgiveness doesn't begin until that justice is given to the wounded, and at that point, the wrongdoer achieves a level of respect for taking responsibility rather than remaining an insensitive bully who hides behind cowardice. Good manners such as using "please", "thank you", and "I'm sorry" convey caring. We use them too infrequently and they should especially be used for those we love.

It is that level of graciousness that sets a far different tone in a family than constant criticism, which is more the norm in families. You especially see it on the *Dr. Phil Show*, the *Jerry Springer Show*, and other dysfunctional family counseling types of shows. That kind, rational person, who is the focus of the show, explaining the problem in a solo interview before the camera turns into a ranting, indignant, outraged monster once the family member joins the group. We the parents set the tone. And the basic tone of any relationship should be politeness, compassion, and appreciation. Dr. Phil says for every hurtful criticism you level at your child it takes ten *atta boys* to heal it. How does your game card look? And I mean on a daily basis. As someone who suffered depression and suicidal impulses for years, let me tell you that it is the destructive criticism day in and day out that sends you down that path. Healing and balance must start with us, the parents. We must model what we want to see and to create an atmosphere of growth. You must learn calm and assertive parenting tempered with compassion.

Anger Management

Whenever I hear parents complain that their teen or child is always yelling and arguing with them and that they are victimized, I know there was a model parent or authority figure somewhere nearby in the family. On occasion, a dysfunctional tirade has been established with the parent as a victim and the *child* as a persecutor. But generally, the screaming, yelling, and demanding started long ago in the discipline of the child and this is the end result. To put it crudely, they learned it somewhere and that somewhere—99 times out of 100—was at home. If you don't like it, it is time you stopped doing it and came to a truce, a cease-fire. I don't like my home life to be full of strife. In both of my failed marriages there was no yelling except for on the rare occasion. The world outside provides me with enough upheaval without having it in my home, and it wasn't something either of my husbands found comfort in. We grew apart over other issues. I grew up with constant strain and tension, with my parents yelling, hitting us with belts, and grounding us, and unfortunately that continues in so many families. You can stop it. I made the rule in my house and you can also. No more yelling. You must act with intelligence and strive to be cool and calm. I've been upset enough at times to take time out for myself to calm down before resolving the issue. You ask your children to do that on the playground when they are so little, there is no reason you can't do it as an adult.

The common perception of anger as I have heard Dr. Phil say, is that it really is a mask for other emotions. The three he names are fear, hurt, and frustration. If you can start substituting those words for *anger* you can get to the problem and solve it better. *Anger* is a lashing out, an aggression resulting from one of those emotions. I believe there are two other motives behind anger. The fourth one is to quell anxiety. Of course you could say this is fear based, but when I see some *rageholics*, they can be anxious about something and feel out of control in aspects of their lives and they repeatedly and daily go through these anger outbursts over trivial things. They are releasing the pent up anxiety that keeps flushing through them. Sadly, the targets, who may be their children, take on the fault for these outbursts. It took me a long time to realize my parents were usually very anxious about their finances. Any small incident that seemed to pile on more pressure would send them into snapping and snipping at any of us kids.

A fifth motive behind anger is *sadism,* a pleasure in hurting others, in having power over another to feel superior. If the rest of the world isn't giving you what you need emotionally, you can lash out and take pleasure in the power of being able to cause the pain in them that others cause in you. We don't like to acknowledge this but it is there. Sadly, some therapists avoid, assist, and enable sadists or abusers, who of course, blame their victims. We are horrified when this goes to the point of criminal behavior but it can start in small ways. It starts with some people harming their children. It starts out with yelling and throwing things or hitting, shoving, and can degenerate into child abuse.

Rule number one has to be that verbal and emotional assaults are no longer tolerated. For some people this will eliminate the majority of their daily interactions. They have gotten used to being assaultive and vent this way because it makes them feel self righteous and validated. They vent this way, they feel self righteous and validated. It

Chapter 4 Preparing the Ground for the Garden

costs the recipients and abusers alike emotionally, and those costs go on for years. It is a habit, and sadly one they most likely endured while young. We all have to work on it in some degree or another. But excuses and explanations are meaningless. You don't get to go up to someone on the street and hit them, so now you don't get to assault the young person who is your offspring. This is the next evolution in parenting. This is our job. I remember my parents seeming to enjoy watching us cry and cringe from the belt beatings. They felt validated in their retribution of some insult or harm to them or their things. Justice was being done. But was it? Are we any better criticizing and judging our children's failures? A failure needs to be an opportunity to try again, to come up with a new approach, for us to lend support during a moment of difficulty. It teaches how to be the person we need to be when we face failure or the success we are striving to obtain.

I have a very distant cousin, Thomas, who considers himself to be very upstanding and moral. He has served in the military, he has done missionary work with his church, and he has lead men's groups in his church. Dr. Phil has done a number of shows in which one of the participants is what he calls "a right fighter". They not only have to be right, they have to make sure that they have shoved you into the dirt and made you wrong. Then they feel self righteous and validated. We all know them; you say the sky is blue, they say technically it isn't, it is the atmosphere, or whatever. You are never right and they have to make sure you know it. Whatever you say or whatever opinion you have, theirs is superior and correct and yours is inferior and wrong. The implication is that you are inferior and they are superior.

Thomas is a right fighter. I doubt that a day goes by when he isn't crushing someone with his superior intellect and positions. But Thomas is a lonely man. People avoid him; he has destroyed almost all of his relationships. He has cried from the loneliness. He is a workaholic; his wife is frightened of him, as is his son, Alex. Thomas doesn't see that he has become the bully like the ones that used to terrorize him as a child. He is always punishing his son for any and all perceived infractions, large or small. As a young man ready to go off to college, Alex is failing school miserably. More of an artistic sort, Alex doesn't turn in homework and he exhibits strong symptoms of withdrawal and depression. Anyone looking at the situation knows Alex will never do enough or be enough for his father. Sadly, his father sees his constant criticism and judgment as constructive. How can you improve if you don't know where you are failing, right? This is the tendency of parents trying to raise their young adults and teens. What they fail to note is that these young people are in perhaps the biggest part of their lives when mistakes are routine and must happen. They are starting to assume adult responsibilities while juggling complex social demands, parent demands, and life demands. They are judged brutally by their high school peers. They have to build barriers to survive and come across as cool and remote. I remember having a talk with my youngest son, Richard, about how critical parents and teachers seem to be in these high school years. Gone is the cutesy adult encouragement of elementary school days and present are the prison warden attitudes. I told him I get how harsh life is for them. I understand how hurtful these years are and how everyone has to build a wall of indifference to save their wounded souls and feelings. He looked at me, stunned and speechless. Don't we all at that age think we are hiding things so well? And the bottom line is that they are. Without fail, parents complain that they feel left out of their teen's world, closed off. At almost every parent ed course I've attended, a comment is made that conversations with their teens are grunts or one-word answers. "How was your day?" a parent will ask. "Good" is the teen response. "Anything wrong?" a parent inquires. "No" is the typical response.

But what other response would you expect if you were attacked or criticized for your thoughts and beliefs? That is what we tend to do as parents. I love asking my sons for their opinions. I will ask how they like a new recipe I tried or what I could add or detract from it. I'll ask about their favorite actor, singer, or musical preference. I was so surprised to find out that my youngest son liked jazz. What do they think of the latest Hollywood scandal or the latest political scandal? If you talk to them as you would to a friend or someone you meet at a party, you will get answers and they will open up to you.

Especially if your responses aren't to criticize their opinions! I think my youngest son, Richard, is a bit of a radical sometimes in his beliefs, but I remember being just as passionate at his age. I'll tell him, "the other side to that is blah, blah, but I think you have a valid point there." It doesn't mean I have to agree with him but he needs to be validated even if his opinion is different. They will hear what you said and maybe mull it over because you are their model. More critically, you have taught them respect. I hear so many parents say they feel disrespected. Without exception, they have modeled that and it doesn't feel good when it comes back at them. If you are calm and respectful, you can get your point across and they will hear it a lot more than if you put them down as being stupid or naïve.

I have attended a popular play around the country, *Menopause the Musical* in which four women of various backgrounds become friends when they happen to meet at a sale in Bloomingdale's in New York. One woman is an attorney, another is an aging soap opera actress, a third is a middle-aged hippie earth mother type, and the fourth is a housewife from the Midwest attending a convention in New York with her husband, who is a professional. In one song they all lament the criticisms from their own mothers who treated them as if they were still children. If you have experienced that, and it sure resonates with a lot of people, you know that there isn't a give and take relationship and you get the hurt of not being validated by your parents even when you are so old that you have grown children yourself. Our role should be less "judge and jury" and more as a supporter, the Counselor role in Jim Fay's parenting books. Dr. Phil says that we all need a person in our life, whether it is a parent or mate, who is our "a soft place to fall." Are you a soft place to fall for your teen or young adult?

How do we change the old role of judge and criticizer? We do it by substituting criticism with encouragement and support. For example, I was recently teaching a young 20-year-old woman, Cindy, to drive. Cindy was the much-loved only child of a very strong willed and capable single mother, Lydia. Many people would see Lydia as a control freak who was very involved with her daughter's Girl Scout Troop, school, and life in general. She adored her daughter to the point of great fear and anxiety that came across as controlling. Lydia didn't want her daughter to suffer or fail in life's challenges or situations and was trying to do everything for Cindy. Cindy was bright and sweet, but a nervous wreck from her mother's constant protection that drifted from being *helping* to being *interfering* at times. Cindy wound up moving away to go to school to get a little breathing room. Cindy had never learned to drive. She had gotten her permit at 15½ years old as most teens did. But when it came time to drive with

Chapter 4 Preparing the Ground for the Garden

her mother, one lesson left her shattered with her mother's constant worry and direction. She refused to drive with her mother ever again. As I explained to Cindy, the same thing happened when I drove with my father. I remember the exact block we were driving down when we heard the harsh sound of fire engine horns behind me a block away. To add more than terror to this situation, this was back in the day when we learned to drive stick shifts, so there was a lot to learn with the brake, clutch, and gas pedals. I looked in my rear view mirror to see where the truck was and tried to figure out where to pull over on the side of the street. During this whole time, my father was yelling at me to pull over, pull over, pull over! I heard his panic and fear but it wasn't helping me or giving me a chance to handle the situation, which was new to me. I did pull over, the fire engine went by and I was an emotional mess. I refused to ever drive with him again. My mother had a great way of laughing when she got nervous, like she was participating in a sit-com. I would immediately wonder what I was doing wrong, but nervous laughter was a much better way of learning for me than my father's yelling. The hidden message was that she believed I could do it given a little time.

When Cindy first started driving, we did the usual thing of going to the local school parking lot. It was after hours in the early evening time of late fall. There were no cars and I foolishly thought that because Lydia had sent Cindy out with several driving schools after Cindy refused to drive with her mother that it would be a matter of just refreshing rusty driving skills. We also were under time constraints. Cindy wanted to get her driver's license because she was leaving the area. She was headed to the opposite coast to transfer to a school she had always wanted to attend. That was all going to happen in less than three months. Given her level of fear, she just didn't think she would accomplish this. And in the parking lot, I realized that she was very much a new beginner with few skills to draw on from the past.

I had seen from working with Justin that a lot of the work was in teaching himself to play new tapes in his mind of hope and self-confidence. In psychology, we used to say that the internal dialogue that people run and that creates their world gets programmed into them through their parents, and it is like running music tapes over and over. We repeat to ourselves what others have said or what we have said to ourselves. Today it would be CDs instead of tapes, but the idea is that we play them over and over. It is critical to get new messages into the dialogue in our heads. The purpose behind that is that you want the new tapes to become a self-filling prophecy. We will experience what we are playing. We create most of our reality and often it comes from what others have said to us and not from the messages we choose to play.

I let Cindy drive around and around the parking lot. I knew part of it was that she had to develop a relationship with me. Would I be critical like her mom? I stayed calm, let her make some decisions as to which set of parking space markers to go around, and finally we got out onto the street of our very quiet neighborhood. I explained that she was building a number of skill sets, how to take guidance from me, how to manage the car, and how to read other drivers and their intentions. There was a lot of hand and eye coordination going on and after a while the brain would have it locked into an automatic reaction, but for the moment we are building the skill set. I told her to be kind to herself. It is a lot and we were finding our way with what was comfortable for her brain.

We weren't in any real traffic the next time either. I had to get her used to the occasional car that came up behind her. We practiced right hand turns that she initially hated. I explained we would do them over and over until her brain was getting automatic with it. Whenever she did something good, I explained how that execution was good. If there was a mistake, we figured out how it could be improved upon and that everyone is different. After a while, she began to look at how to improve on her performance and what went wrong with a situation. She learned to trust me, and what was more important was that I trusted her. I had faith in her. Don't we all crave that type of belief in who we are and what we are doing? My mantra was, "Excellent, now that you have pretty much mastered that, let's move onto a new skill and build on success." Always, we were building on success.

I heard a story once that Thomas Edison made over 1000 attempts at creating the light bulb. When they were referred to as his failures, his reply was that they weren't. He had learned 1000 ways how <u>not</u> to make a light bulb. As I told Justin when he was learning to drive, it is all a video game; you figure out how to master the level and move to the next. It got to the point where Cindy was excited to drive and since she was my fourth student, I was learning how to be a better teacher. I learned what the examiners were looking for and how to build on the driving skills I now take for granted. Some skills have become so automatic that we forget what it was like long ago when it was all new. As parents we then hold the new learners to our experienced standard as if it is so easy and the fault must be in our teen our adult child. If we are to develop resilience in our young adults, we must let them learn from their mistakes and celebrate their mastery no matter how long the process takes or how minute the apparent advancement. Often skill sets need to *marinate* overnight in the brain to form the new pathways needed to execute them more smoothly the next time. At least, that is how it seems to me in my observations.

All of this came to a huge test on the day of Cindy's driver's exam. As luck would have it, I had the chance to be interviewed on my topic and book on a local TV talk show. It was last minute but a huge opportunity for me. We couldn't cancel her test as she was packing to move out of state. There wouldn't be time for another test. But I always have a plan B and plan C and, if lucky, a plan D. We agreed that Justin would drive her to and from her test, since it was at the same time as my TV interview. If she didn't pass, we would discuss ways in which she could return here to retake it or how to practice on her visits home and retake it. The permit lasted a year and she had no trouble passing the written part. I found it rather touching that Justin who only two years earlier had taken this test three times, was now driving someone else who was in his shoes from just the recent past.

Her test was at 2:00 p.m. I had to leave for my interview at 1:30 and she and Justin would leave from my home at 1:30 also. We agreed that I would pick her up that morning at around 11:00 and we would do some practice driving around the neighborhood of the Department of Motor Vehicles (DMV) so it felt familiar. We had practiced many times. Cindy was staying at an apartment near her school, about 45 minutes from my house. It was good practice to get her driving the various streets before hitting the highway and getting in some highway practice. I had noticed on a previous driving experience that when one street came to a dead end and two lanes turned left and one turned right, Cindy had trouble staying in her lane on the left turn. I had corrected her as she drifted from the inner left lane to the outer lane while

Chapter 4 Preparing the Ground for the Garden

in the intersection. I assumed that she understood. I find that as I coach and parent, I learn as much as my teens or parents are learning. Cindy had not quite understood. I had not verbalized it or drawn it out for her sufficiently. Again, she was in the inner left lane, turning. She started to drift into the outer left turn lane in the intersection. We experienced drivers know that this causes a problem if someone is speeding up to make the left turn in the outer lane because they will be in our blind spot and they are expecting you to stay in your lane through the turn. I quickly told her to stay in her lane, that she was drifting, and she was a bit flustered, not quite understanding what I was saying again. I realized too late that she wasn't seeing how the lane continued. In the meantime, the woman behind her saw her drifting outward and, assuming she would continue into the outer lane, tried to pass her on the turn. The woman was in her blind spot on the driver's side so that when Cindy tried to return to her inner lane, the two cars scrapped together.

We pulled over as Cindy was almost in tears saying, "This is a bad omen, it can't be happening!" Of course, I just about thought the same thing! But I calmed her down and said, "Let me handle this," and got out to talk to the woman. We both agreed to keep it off our insurance and saw that there was minor damage to both of our older cars and exchanged information. I explained that Cindy was just learning to drive. The other woman looked like a grandmother and gently asked if this was her first lesson. I said no but she was learning. She seemed sympathetic and commented she was sorry that I seemed to have a worse scrap than she did. You never know if people will be nice to you at the time of an incident and then allege horrific damage and injury afterwards, but I took it at face value. I went back to my car. Cindy was distraught. I told her that she had just experienced a surge of adrenalin and I would drive us to the DMV neighborhood while it washed through her. She was downcast and very upset.

I could have yelled at her and really vented, but how would that help? This is where parents have to go to work as Jim Fay's Counselors. I pointed out that she now knows how to handle an accident and to understand that it is a very emotional time due to the adrenalin rush. We talked about what went right and what went wrong. I explained the woman was wrong to pass, I had been wrong not to have gone over those turns better, and she was wrong in drifting, but we all learned and no one was hurt. We agreed that we would only tell her mother if the other driver didn't let it go as promised and contacted us, as I knew that was at the top of her worry chart. This was a golden opportunity to discuss that life happens. I explained that this wasn't so much an omen as an advanced life-learning lesson. Even that approach wasn't raising her spirits much so I finally told her that if I didn't think she could do it or she wasn't a safe beginner driver, I would not let be letting her take her test that day. I believed in her and we would get through this. Suddenly she seemed to pull herself together. Parents, these are the moments you have to make an impression, and don't you blow it! I was modeling calmness but inside I felt a bit shaken, too. In Cesar Millan's *Dog Whisperer* language, no matter what, you must remain a calm, assertive presence. In time, it will be the natural way for you to be. Isn't that much better than the out of control, emotional nut case that most of us are used to being? And the more you practice remaining calm, the easier it becomes. I certainly didn't need to be an emotional mess for my interview and I wasn't. The situation was calmly handled and let go.

We drove to the DMV neighborhood and she drove like a dream. As we headed back to meet Justin, she asked that we not tell him. That was fine with me. We both preferred to deal with any further fallout from the incident when that time came. Right then, we both needed to be calm and in top form. I did my TV interview, live of course, and it went well but the whole time I was wondering how her test was going. I was as ready, as I had been with my sons and Justin before their tests, to console her and bring out plan B or plan C should she not make it. Because I was in a TV studio, I wasn't getting cell phone reception. As soon as I was far enough away after the interview, I called. She had passed!

She had learned she could pass a test that she had feared for years and that she could recover from disasters and still do well. Is that not a great day? If it had been my parents overseeing something like that, I would have heard a huge amount of criticism for the accident and probably guarded praise like, "You were just lucky you passed." I never believed in me because my parents never seemed to believe in me, although I heard many years later that real praise was given about me by them to friends and family behind my back. That is not good. Don't assume your teen or young adult knows. They look to you for how to evaluate their performances in gathering skill sets and life lessons.

And how did Lydia react to the news? I was probably more proud of Lydia than anyone. She was someone who had a tendency to give out guarded praise that could sound like disappointment. But she could also provide real praise and pride in her daughter, but you couldn't be sure which it would be at any given time. Cindy had told her mother for several years that she didn't want to drive until she had surgery to correct some minor vision problems. So when Cindy told Lydia, in front of many friends a few weeks after passing, Lydia reassured her daughter that had she had the surgery sooner she would have had her license at the same time as her friends. There was no backhanded comment such as, "Why did it take so long?" or anything in that vein, as so many parents might say. We celebrated the success and did not diminish it. Along with no more anger toward our young adults, we must insist on no more diminishing their accomplishments. After all, if life is a video game; the fact that you made it to a new level is a victory not diminished by all the trials and errors along the way. ✑

Chapter 5 Planting the Seeds of Success

Preparing the ground is critical not only for success in launching our teens and young adults, but also to have the warm, loving relationship we all dreamed of when they were born. We need to recognize our anger as being hurt, fear, and frustration at the very least, and in severe cases as being abuse. Anger management classes are available. I am always shocked when therapists don't require their more physical and explosive clients to go to anger management classes. As an attorney, I find it sad that judges can require it in their rulings but mental health professionals don't seem quite as inclined. Once again, in the words of Cesar Millan, the Dog Whisperer, we need to bring a calm, assertive energy to our parenting. Violent outbursts, while understandable at times, are not acceptable as a day-to-day strategy. I often watch Dr. Phil's show and am horrified that he sits by while family members go at each other in anger. At the very least, you won't solve things until you take out the anger and talk in a reasonable and calm manner. This is about problem solving, not about battles of ego in an effort to be right or hurl emotions at each other. In my humble opinion, Dr. Phil needs to stop the outbursts and demand civility. These people need to learn to argue in a calm, civil manner that promotes solutions, not abusively, and often parents need to do the same.

Dreams, Visualizations, and Self-fulfilling Prophecies

In our first step, we are dealing with our anger and keeping it out of the relationship. We are offering encouragement and praise and now let's add the seeds to our prepared garden. There are many books on how our intentions, our action-moving forward, and visualizing our future situation determines our life story. *Creative Visualization* by Shakti Gawain gives exercises, meditations, and lessons in creating what you want in life through visualization. *Excuse Me, Your Life is Waiting* by Lynn Grabhorn explains that if you immerse yourself in the feelings of what you want, it creates a law of attraction bringing you the outcome you want. *The Secret* by Rhonda Byrne is currently a favorite on these ideas of the law of attraction and the power of intent. Tony Robbins says in his inspirational tapes that the brain is very powerful and whatever it focuses it on will bring about the experiences being perceived. He uses an exercise wherein you are to play a memory game. He will name a color and within five seconds you are to scan your surroundings and memorize all that you see of that color. For example, you are to memorize all that is the color green. Five seconds later you close your eyes and name everything you saw that was brown. That's right, brown. When you open your eyes, you will be amazed at all the brown you missed. But you were focused on green and that is why you missed the brown. If we travel this world looking for the negative experiences, that is what we will *see* the most of in the world and in our lives.

Failure to Launch: How to Get Your Teens and Young Adults to Independence

The seeds you plant in your adult child can be ones of success or ones of suspected failure. There were studies in the 1960's by Robert Rosenthal and Lenore Jacobson on the impact of self-fulfilling prophecies. In their landmark 1968 study, they tested a class of elementary school children for intelligence. They then took the scores of the students and assigned them to other students. If a child the teacher thought was bright had a low score, they told the teacher that the child was an overachiever and not really as smart as one thought. Similarly, for those children who were generally average but now had high scores on the test, the teacher was told those students were late bloomers and gifted. At the end of the year, they retested the kids and the scores tended to match the statements made to the teacher regarding those children. In short, a child who started out with an average IQ but was said to be gifted by the end of the year was testing closer to gifted. The reverse was happening to the ones who tested well but were said not to be so bright, in that they tested poorly at the end of the year on average. The biggest factor was the perception of the teacher and not the innate intelligence or abilities of the child. This had huge implications for children of color who suffered from stereotypes of low intelligence. Many studies have been done since confirming this phenomenon. I think it is interesting to note that these were children who looked for validation and confirmation from others. As we become adults we can reduce our experiences with people who are projecting these poor beliefs on us and fight back with our own experiences and data, but at that young age when we look to adults as authority figures and people we love, we tend to take their valuations of us as reality. This is why it is so important to watch what is said to your young adult and your teen. They are vulnerable to our judgments. Remember, as Dr. Phil says, it takes ten *atta boys* to make up for one hurtful criticism.

Don't look at your young adult as a failure. In Justin's case, he had so many strikes against him. He had been labeled as having learning disabilities and he had no role model in his parents to be a successful employee. But he dreamed it and looked for it in celebrities and movies. His aunt Sara had complained to me while he was living with her that all she wanted was for him to get a full-time job with benefits, a driver's license, a place of his own, and to go to college. In three years, all that she had wanted for him has come true, but not as she had envisioned it and not with her help. Those were the things Justin wanted also, and by deciding he could have those things, we made it happen. Tony Robbins believes in "massive action" and I believe he is right. You start to move toward those dreams and sometimes they take on a life of their own and propel you forward to the next move.

I have a friend who is a social worker with the state taking care of abused children. She sees horrible things done to these children from abuse to neglect. She told me once that she would love to get a grant to teach these kids to learn how to dream. They live their lives waiting to be victimized or hoping for a day without the victimizing. They have no dreams, no hope, and no belief that there is something better for them. This happens for other people, not just the abused. I suffered as a teen for years from depression. The constant criticism and judgment drove me to a suicide attempt and suicidal depression. I saw nothing hopeful in my life path. Before attending a Tony Robbins seminar that taught me how to drive away those depressive patterns of thinking, I attended a past lives seminar with one of my favorite authors, Brian Weiss, who wrote *Many Lives, Many Masters*. In one exercise, we exchanged a small item—car keys, a piece of jewelry, or something—with a person we didn't know sitting nearby. Brian Weiss was a psychiatrist who used hypnosis to treat some of his patients, and in

32

Chapter 5 Planting the Seeds of Success

his seminar he hypnotized us while we held the objects of our partners. We were to simply let whatever images came up emerge. He brought us out of the exercise and we then exchanged the *visions* we had had with our class partners. A large number of people seemed to have seen aspects of the other person's life in their visions. I was able to see the mountains and the bald eagles flying in what turned out to be my partner's favorite place to hike on his and his wife's anniversary. But when it was his turn, he said he simply saw a long road gently going up and down into the far distance and there was nothing around, no landscape, and no scenery. All he saw was the road. With a start, I realized that it was how I envisioned my life. I saw and lived life as an empty emotional landscape where you stay on the road until you get to the end of life. That was how I had survived my childhood and teen years and that still was my self-fulfilling prophecy. I now have populated that emotional landscape to the hilt with beautiful scenery and loving moments and happiness with friends and family. Teach your teen and young adult to dream, and don't let your fears pollute their lives. Much of the great stories and adventures in our lives and our children's lives come from the journey to attaining our dreams. Not the end attainment, but the journey. Always build new dreams. They are the life we all live.

Notice that I did not say what the dream should be. Sometimes we fear for the risks that our young adult wants to take. Maybe they want to move far away or take on a career such as fire fighting or police work that is dangerous. It isn't our job to make them live for us. We can voice our concern, but after that it is up to them to decide how to proceed and up to us to make peace within ourselves with their choice. This speaks to the issue of boundaries, which we will discuss. We all have the right to make our choices and the people we love need to respect that. I have watched parents try to get their young adults to take on careers that will bring status to the parents or the kind of job security that makes the parents feel secure. Usually, when parents succeed in controlling their child's future like this, they have an unhappy young adult trudging along in a life that is not of their own choice and making. One example that comes to mind is a young man who wanted to enter the movie business either as a producer or in some capacity other than acting. When he speaks about movies, he is passionate and happy. But his parents forbade that he go that way in college; they demanded that since they were paying for college he get a degree in business. He seemed deflated but, loving his parents, he is living his life to make them feel secure about his future. There is no reason why he can't get that business degree and use it in the entertainment arena. But the fear of the parents that life in that industry is so tenuous overshadows his dream and quite frankly is a wrong assumption on their part. We need to help our young adults to be realistic in how to accomplish their dreams. Eventually, they will have to pay their bills and most likely support a family, but it can be done with a bit of thought and research to have the dream and the job. To have the dream is the start of finding out who they are.

Create a Willing Spirit

Dr. Phil likes to say that you don't just get rid of one habit, you replace it with another. Once you replace the usual tendency to criticize and judge with exploring and supporting, the relationship becomes more positive. Once it is more positive, you both can accomplish more.

One element that both Tony Robbins and Robert Kiyosaki, author of *Rich Dad, Poor Dad*, both espouse is a can-do philosophy. As I recall from listening to Robert Kiyosaki's book on tape, he had a birth father and a stepfather. His birth father was highly educated but had the "Poor Dad" attitude toward money. The other father never finished 8th grade but was much wealthier because he had a "Rich Dad" attitude toward money. The book describes six lessons of how to think like a "Rich Dad" and a lot of it includes life attitudes and approaches in whether we give up control and become victims to the whims of life or take control and see the opportunities in the challenges that life places before us. One example Robert Kiyosaki uses is that of the two fathers passing an expensive car on the street. The "Poor Dad" is likely to say, "I can't afford that." Desiring the car, the "Rich Dad" will say, "How can I afford that?" These are two different views, two different lives and outcomes. You can also say this is the law of attraction, a self-fulfilling prophecy set in motion. The difference is that it begins the journey for the "Rich Dad" and it is the end of the journey for the "Poor Dad".

Tony Robbins says that if we think of the brain as a computer, what we ask of it is critical. If you ask, "Why can't I ever get ahead?" the brain will start answering all the reasons you <u>can't</u>, and many times it answers with things you might have heard from the significant adults in your world. It may say, "You're not smart enough, you're not educated enough, you are always unlucky, you haven't got what it takes, etc." All of these narrow your choices and your dreams. If you ask, "How can I get ahead?" your brain will start to come up with ideas about how you can get ahead, and as you act on them and learn from them, you will find you are moving down the road to getting ahead. The journey begins or ends with your questions. That has been the most remarkable experience for me and I have watched it unfold over and over for myself and others.

It was so hard for Justin to learn to drive. He said his mother, stepfather, and grandfather had all tried to teach him and gave up. He was doubtful it could happen. In short, the journey had ended. I didn't know if it could be done. After all, three people had tried and the common denominator was Justin, right? But in true Tony Robbins fashion, I said, "Let's give it a shot. How can we make this happen?" After all, maybe his family members weren't patient or maybe he needed to mature a bit; in short, there were a number of reasons that it hadn't worked before. It took four attempts to get his permit but each time we resolved to do it again. When he passed, we both realized that we each had learned a lot. I began to understand in this video game-like challenge of getting the permit just how the test worked and how to be successful at the test. Justin learned to persevere, and not to give up and accept the judgments of others about him or his abilities. In the face of self-fulfilling prophecies, we can decide not to accept those perceptions others have of us. We can give up our power or find our way with the love and support of those who believe in us. Even in job-hunting for Justin, I would find out his interests and propose a path of research. He was interested in travel and he had been in ROTC (Reserve Officers' Training Corps) in high school. I asked if he would like to try airport security. He immediately said he couldn't do that, he wouldn't know how. This was a fairly common response to new things for him. His brain was immediately programmed to "how come that wouldn't work" mode. So my job was as much to get him to think of how it could work as it was to help him check out the possibility at hand.

Chapter 5 Planting the Seeds of Success

He filled out the application online and got a call for the position. We assumed it was an interview. It turned out to be a test which involved looking at a jumble of items on a screen in rapid succession and trying to discern potentially dangerous items. He didn't pass. One of the instructors told him that typically it takes three tests before people pass. However, having done it once, he was uninterested. Being more of a people person, rote screening did not appeal to him. But he had given it a shot and learned something about the profession and himself and that was a good thing. It wasn't long before he was trying things and figuring out how to do the research, what to get out of the potential field, and how to evaluate it in terms of his strengths. When we make tasks and experiences about the success or failure of the person, we all are less inclined to attempt new things. When we make it about research and learning through experience, the pressure is off. One's self esteem is not at risk. In fact, it adds to one's life experience and self esteem to give it a try. Taking a calculated risk is a good thing. We have to learn about what does and doesn't work for us. An excellent book for finding out one's strengths is *Strength Finder 2.0* by Tom Rath. It comes with a code that you access online to get the test. It is an interesting test that takes about 15 to 20 minutes. From that you learn what your top five strengths are and in the book it directs you to jobs and careers that would be a good match for you. But we didn't have that resource at that time. Ours was more of a trial and error approach of what would and wouldn't work. It still netted a lot of information and is a good place to start.

My oldest son, Adam, spent his first two years of college in San Diego. Like most freshman coming from the cooler climes of northern California, the prospect of an endless summer seemed tantalizing. Adam is very much a people person like I am. But after two years he felt that he was totally mismatched. He found the people to be more status conscious and materialistically driven than he was. The general education requirements were boring him. He was tired of teaching associates who had little or no ability to teach. It has become common practice of many universities to employ teaching assistants for general education classes to save professors time to research and write. As consumers, parents need to demand that professionals teach these very expensive classes, but that is another book altogether. Adam was barely pulling a "C" average and was unhappy. Now, many parents would urge their student to persevere. He's half done, he's not failing, and it's a good school, good climate, so why pull up to leave? He had loved visiting his friends up the coast in Santa Barbara, California, which is less than two hours north of Los Angeles. He said he regretted not trying to go to the University of California there. I encouraged him to transfer. He went through the process only to find out that they required a 2.8 grade point average to get into the business major there. His grade point average wasn't quite there. Remember, when we hit a challenge or obstacle, start asking "how can I get past this?" One plan we came up with as to how he could make it happen was for him to go to the community college in that town to build up his grade point average (GPA) and get some of the general education requirements behind him. He came to a point where he asked me for some coaching. Was he being foolish? Should he stay in San Diego? What if he couldn't get his GPA up to get into a business major? Would he be going to school a lot longer than he wanted? I told him to listen to his heart. I loved visiting him in San Diego. I have friends there, I love the heat and the ambiance, but if he didn't feel happy there and I had heard that several times in the two years he wasn't happy there, then it wasn't for him. If he didn't get his GPA up at the community college enough to transfer, he would still be working toward the units needed to graduate. Perhaps he would also find that just visiting a place like Santa Barbara and living there were two very different critters and he'd return to San Diego after a leave of absence with a fresh perspective. Nothing is lost really. This is teaching him that he needs to learn to follow his instincts and take the risks to learn who he is. In all of this, we parents need to stop being lazy. All too frequently, we lay out game plans that ask little of us. It would have been nice to have him go straight through one college with few moves, with the stability of knowing where he was, but our real goal as parents is to produce an adaptable, grown adult. Security is nice but if we make our security the driving factor for our lives, we lose the ability to adapt. For example, in my generation we were encouraged to shoot for one job for the rest of our life, but then if that job or career is gone, as is happening in this day and age, you have a very lost adult. Security has to come from knowing you can adapt to changing everything. That means acquiring many skill sets and knowing that you can do this. In this case, he would learn how to navigate different education institutions, the ins and outs of moving, how to make new friends, get oriented in a new city, etc. We always forget they don't have the adult skill sets we have. They need to acquire them through life experience.

Adam moved and began his schooling in Santa Barbara. He loved it. He felt at home. But his GPA was not enough to transfer into a business major. We formulated many plans to help him succeed. We looked at whether or not he might want to go work for his uncle in Los Angeles. He had spent a summer working at his uncle's clothing company and became quite excited working in the fashion industry. He was thirsty for knowledge and his uncle and partner in the business rotated Adam through the various departments to get him to know all aspects of the business. Being more of a hands on, real world type learner, this suited him well. College had been more esoteric and unrelated to life for the most part and that just wasn't something that he found interesting or challenging. In fact, this is the major complaint that many high school students and college students have about education. It isn't relevant to the real world. He thought about his options for a while. I myself have had periods in and out of college so I was a role model for it being something he could pick up later if he wanted. I encourage all my parent clients not to panic if their student wants to take a breather to get oriented in life and go to college when it seems right. College needs to fit hand in hand with real world job experiences. He concluded that he wanted that Bachelor's degree, and since he had momentum, he'd see it through.

Before he moved there, we looked at places and colleges that might better suit him. He had lived and worked in L.A. for that summer with his uncle's business and there were many college choices there. But his heart was really in Santa Barbara. Now one of the things I'm very big on is having multiple plans. So often we pick one path and put all of our stock in that plan without a fallback plan should the chosen one not work out. Defeated, we fall into a comfort zone and give up our dreams for safe and secure day-to-day living. We settle and live life without passion and assume that at best, we should be happy for crumbs of happiness. I also believe that sometimes we need to be aware of our destiny, our happiness giving us subtle signs to follow. Those signs may come with a few obstacles but sometimes those are the lessons we need to prepare us for our achieving our dreams. Adam still wanted to go to the UC in Santa Barbara and he didn't give up that dream even though he made preparations to transfer to other schools. There was no guarantee that he could get in. As luck would have it, he stumbled on a new counselor at UC who had been the lead counselor at one time and was very seasoned in helping others. He advised Adam to try to enter in with a different major, like political science, that would be a good fit but have a lower

Chapter 5 Planting the Seeds of Success

GPA requirement, and he told Adam that he was more than qualified to get into the school. Additionally, the political science major was experiencing fewer transfers than they had hoped, so the chances of getting in were very high. Even Adam's brother commented that he thought Adam could make a great career out of politics, even more so than business. I myself have worked in politics and for political campaigns. The apple might not be falling far from the tree but I hadn't thought of it. The bottom line was to help him find the life he wants. What is important is to formulate ideas, work them until we move forward, or drop them. If you can get your young adult to start thinking in those terms, you are creating a problem solver, a creative person who finds solutions.

What I am telling you is to be open to many possibilities and encourage exploration. Take those first steps forward; keep moving forward and look for challenges as opportunities. Remember what we said earlier about the brain? You have to get your brain to respond to the question, "How can I make this happen?" Ask that question over and over and over as you move forward. Change tactics if need be. Collect information as you go. Why? To better adapt to facts and circumstances and develop a skill set of how to deal with those apparent obstacles as opportunities with treasures waiting for you to discover.

Plan B

When I was married to my sons' father, he had dreamed in college of becoming an astronomer. It was his heart and passion. But it was the time of the Viet Nam war and his draft number was up. Being a very intelligent man, his parents knew if he went to medical school, his draft status would be deferred. He entered medical school to become the doctor his parents would be so proud of. Being loving parents, they wanted his older brother to become a dentist and thus both of their sons would have secure careers with good income and good status. But that career absolutely did not fit with his brother's personality and he wound up going into the clothing business and becoming a multi-millionaire. He achieved what they wanted but in a manner that was closer to his dreams and abilities. Who could have thought of that as a career for him? I warned my sons not to let their grandparents dictate a profession to them as I knew they would. I wanted my boys to understand that what they become is their choice. Their grandparents were well meaning but survival was the dictate in their generation. It is important to note that although their father was a successful doctor, his real love remained astronomy. He was, in a sense, a square peg in a round hole. He hoped for early retirement. His brother in the meantime had found his passion with a good income and life style to match. You can achieve security and a good career by following your dreams.

One evening my sons came home from dinner with the grandparents in a shocked and incredulous state. Their grandparents had determined that the oldest, Adam should be a lawyer and the youngest, Richard, should be an accountant. These are both great professions. After all, I'm a lawyer and I love it. But Adam's temperament did not strike me as that of a lawyer. It could happen, they were young, but Adam did not like writing which is a key component to being a lawyer. Adam was a natural salesman like his grandfather on his dad's side and my mother. When I had my one and only garage sale that I did with a friend, I was overwhelmed by all the people, the negotiating deals, the demands, the seeming chaos. And there was Adam, at about age 14, helping people and doing something I have since learned is called *bundling*. He would go up to a customer, ask about their interests, whether or not they had children, and then help them to find items that they might like. He would charge a higher price per item unless they bought them as a *bundle* at a reduced price for the lot. I marveled at how easy it was for him to do this. One woman came up to me and said, "You have to get him into sales! He's good!" Not only was he good, he thrived whereas I concluded this would be the last garage sale I would ever do.

Now I'm not saying that Adam may not like being a trial lawyer or a corporate lawyer, even a tax lawyer as he likes math and is really good at it. But he didn't like the reading that would be required or the writing, and unless that changed down the road, none of these aspects would interest him. Ironically, the grandparents chose for Richard, the more studious of the two brothers, the profession of an accountant. Both boys were just shocked at what they felt were occupations that in no way matched their interests. Adam realized as he told me that he just couldn't stand the thought of being a lawyer that he was offending me. I laughed and said it wasn't for everybody, but it worked well for me. Adam had more in common with being an accountant than Richard did and I let them know that they needed to find what worked for them. Their grandparents meant well but an occupation or career will be a prison unless you find a good match for who you are. Still, the grandparents did what so few parents do and need to do. They set an expectation of a field of work, a career. If nothing else, it created a dialogue at an early age about what might work and what might not work. It is really important that we start doing this. We need to ask our teens and young adults, "Where do see yourself in a job and career?" Most fields have multiple types of jobs. If your young adult wants to teach, start exploring what grade level of students and whether they want to work in the private sector or public sector. If they want to go into business ask what sort of companies or institutions would interest them and why. Push for details, for areas to research and think about. With that, my sons' grandparents were on the right path. But again, for the grandparents, their focus was on the end goal and not on the journey to find what would work.

So few of us know what is out there, let alone whether or not it will be a good match. Projections of jobs in the future mean that many of the younger generation will be doing jobs that don't even exist yet. As the markets become more global, is there a safe career that will last most of a lifetime? Hardly. The Michigan town I grew up in had so many car factories and manufacturing of car parts, that it seemed most families had dads employed in a car factory. A man could count on a lifetime job and pleasant retirement as my own father had done. For a young man to get out of high school and go to work in the factory was a lucky move. Now we see people changing jobs in their 50s and creating entire new careers in their 50s once their kids are going off to lead their own lives. I have watched a number of friends lose their retirement packages as companies wiggle for more profits and to just stay alive. I see the same for those people in my hometown whose retirement packages in those car factories are at risk. I have a girlfriend who is an airline pilot and even pilots have watched retirement benefits slip and fall. Security just isn't so secure if you place it in the job and not in your own abilities to adapt and move into something new. But at retirement age, your options are limited. We have to have backup plans these days. We have to learn to be flexible and how to recreate ourselves. Rather than struggle to find the job that will ensure lifetime security, we have to know who we are and what our strengths are,

Chapter 5 Planting the Seeds of Success

what our weaknesses are, and what sort of job areas will be a good fit. We need to teach our young adults how to find out who they are and how to adapt. In all of these searches, there has to be a plan A, the preferred goal that is hopefully one we think we will work best in for the time being and then one or preferably two or three back up plans, the proverbial plan B, plan C, and so on.

Think of it as playing football. You are the coach. You know where you have your major strengths and vulnerabilities as a team and what those factors are in the opposing team. As your team goes out onto the field, you have to watch and see what works and what doesn't and adapt and respond to the changing circumstances. This means that what worked one time may not work once the other team finds out the same things about your team. I took an anthropology class once and the professor was a male who was a professor in both the anthropology department and the nursing department. He had flexibility. There was always the possibility of him advancing in either field or perhaps representing himself as a versatile person in a completely new field. If we can get our teen and young adult to explore the facets of who they are, they will develop resilience to a changing economy and a better sense of who they are and where to look.

When Justin was trying to get a full-time job in retail, we also looked at some other options. We tried the transportation field. He explored jobs in airports, jobs working on trains, everything we could think of minus needing a driver's license. He tried to establish a pet sitting and house sitting business as he loved animals but realized the difficulties in setting up a business. There's a lot to running a business but the biggest problem was not being able to drive to clients. In each of the career pathways, he learned something of the business and the industry and decided if it was right for him. He went to a number of interviews. Originally, he was reluctant to do that if he didn't see himself securing a job. He saw an interview as a commitment to a job by just showing up for the interview. As I pointed out to him as we moved forward in the can-do philosophy, do it for the experience, do it to make connections and know that you are deciding if you really want it. Then again, perhaps the interviewer knew of other opportunities that would work better. He developed confidence. Interviews were Justin's strong point because he is a people person. As stated earlier, in one interview, he was offered a position. But he didn't like the hours and he didn't have a car and they required quite a few night shifts, so it wasn't practical. The fact that he was offered a job built up his confidence and he had learned how to evaluate jobs for his needs. As parents, we forget these important skills in job-hunting that come with experience. Eventually Justin got a full-time job in retail but he had developed a huge set of job seeking skills and the confidence to look outside of his usual scope of jobs. He is still open to new jobs. He has gone from retail to food service all in a matter of three years. He is also now in lower level management which has been his dream for years. He is secure that he can change companies and jobs and do well.

Having plan B or C takes the pressure off of yourself. You have options, you have freedom, and nothing is worse than when you can't leave a job and are treated badly because you haven't allowed yourself backup plans and are now stuck. Flexibility means you can have a quality life, not one of toil and frustration. This moves us into self-development.

S.A.G.E. Parenting

It is very hard for parents in this time period to understand what their job is in relation to raising their teen and young adult. In the past, as I mentioned earlier, our role was very much one of just making sure our children survived. A healthy relationship between adult-child and parent was not part of the goal. If they survived and did not get into trouble, or more accurately, if they brought status to the family, that was a job well done as a parent. It was acceptable to beat or verbally and emotionally wound your child to get compliance. As long as you survived that was enough. Children learned to grow up and leave the abuse. We ran as fast as we could from the personal and emotional destruction.

In underdeveloped nations and our not so distant past, disease is left to cull out the large family numbers. Without antibiotics and vaccines, children die of colds, flu, infections, and many other illnesses. Mothers die in childbirth. Without effective birth control, families are large and death is a real fear for everyone. Parenting has very much been about getting your children to adulthood and settled into reproducing the next generation. For an overwhelmed parent of a large brood of children, the Drill Sergeant parent, as Jim Fay calls them, seemed like a viable parenting style. This authoritarian style is conducive to physical survival but not necessarily to emotional well-being and self-knowledge. It is in fact very impersonal. All that matters is the orders and that those orders are followed. Like in the military where one soldier looks like another, there is no room for personality. It often feels loveless and without feeling. But in another situation, if you were unlucky enough to lose a child, it was understandable that you became, again as Jim Fay says, an over-protective Helicopter parent, always hovering for fear of harm or loss. Both styles have to do with controlling anxiety by controlling behavior and therefore outcomes. But that is an illusion. Following orders leaves the parent and child brittle in new situations, without the ability to adapt. Following rules works only up to a point. But the Helicopter parenting style, when the parent is trying to do for the child or think for the child, leaves crucial life skill sets missing. It is only when you start to mentor or coach or be Jim Fay's Counselor parent that your teen and young adult can begin to develop mastery of adult skill sets and develop a resiliency to an ever-changing world.

Of the three types, the Drill Sergeant and the Helicopter parenting styles are damaging to the inner self, the inner being. They are not viable for emotional survival of your teen and young adult. With all the anti-depressants that we are consuming, we are seeing the price of those poor parenting styles. Life is longer now and we don't merely wish to survive; we wish to thrive. By their children's teen years, parents think that by providing their children with their wants as well as needs and making sure they are good students so that they can go to college, their job is done. What we need to be doing is parenting as S.A.G.E. parents. This has less to do with providing money than providing your teen and adult child with the life and job skills to be independent. College is only a tool and it is not **the** path to independence. In fact, of 100 students entering high school, only 5 of the 11 who do graduate from a four year college will get a job on graduation and be independent. College is not the path to success. It is a tool to use for advancing in a career but the career needs to come first.

Chapter 5 Planting the Seeds of Success

S.A.G.E. is a term I created and it stands for "self accomplished goal era". I invented this term because I want parents to think of themselves in their parenting in this stage as becoming sage-like, wise in how they parent. What we want is to teach our teens and young adults to set their own goals and to teach them the skills to get them to identify the skills they will need. It is about becoming one's true self for our young. More than anything we need them to build in that sense of self-confidence to meet challenges and work them out. We need them to build in that resiliency for a changing world. In the last 100 years we have gone from communicating being done by mail, traveling by horse and buggy, spending most of every day in labor intensive work at home and outside the home to modern labor saving devices, at home entertainment and leisure time, and internet communication. We have no idea how far we can go in the next 100 years and what the landscape will look like. We need to bring S.A.G.E. parenting and all the wisdom we can to building survivors by wit and not just by physical survival.

The principals of S.A.G.E. parenting are much of what we have talked about so far. Calm and assertive leadership is critical. It creates the model for your young adult. Respectful dialogue and listening is a part of that and this is often missing in adult interactions with teens. Another principal is one of creating an atmosphere of talking about plans for independence, helping them to start putting those plans into place with jobs, and working toward those goals in the teen years. They need to be looking at possible jobs and careers early because some or many will get eliminated or further refined as they become familiar with the career pathway. Studies are a part but not all of what parents should focus on in raising their teen and young adult. It shouldn't even be the major part. Career pathway exploration has to take precedence over "going to college" as high school goals.

A largely forgotten principal is letting them take on more adult responsibility with paying bills, doing some banking, and money management. So far, the only adult responsibility we tend to give them is access to a driver's license. That is a start and very important to them becoming independent, but again, not enough. Tied in with listening is helping them to move forward, overcome fears, and problem solve, and giving them praise, especially when something hasn't turned out well. If you can find the silver lining in the cloud, they will learn to do so. Help them learn how to take away the positive in the results as well as figure out what went wrong. This calls for a lot of patience. These are all principals that will drive Drill Sergeant parents and Helicopter parents crazy. These types of people live in anxiety provoking fear, and it is very important that you learn to get out of these roles if you are in them. More than likely you got it from your parents, but it can also arise from your own life experiences. The bottom line is that fear and anxiety are not good. It destroys your ability to be creative and effective. When Cesar Millan talks about a fearful and anxious dog, he tells the dog owner that this is an animal that is out of balance. It isn't healthy for the dog. It is the same for people. Being fearful and anxious can pass to your teen and young adult. Be aware that you are their role model in how you handle situations.

I hear a lot of complaints that teens don't talk to parents. My own biological sons aren't exactly chatterboxes with me but I create opportunities for them to just chat away. You can engage your teen and young adult. Going out to dinner or driving to an event is a good place to start chatting. Respect what they have to say and it gets to be an easier habit to fall into. Remember, you can respectfully agree to disagree. There is no harm in that and at least you have a dialogue and something to think over.

It can also be done if you are bringing something to the table to share with them and teach them. I don't mean *teach* in the sense of telling them what to do or how to do it, but rather in the sense of helping them decipher who they are and what they want. That means having a dialogue. It goes both ways. Whenever I work on a problem with my children or other young adults that I am coaching, I will give my take it on it. How I would do it. I also point out why I make the decisions I make and offer other options. For example, Justin recently brought over his voter's pamphlet to discuss ideas. This is a great way to learn to dialogue. We would talk about what we liked or didn't like about a candidate and we would be respectful. One of the things I learned in law school was the saying, "reasonable minds can differ." If you are a right fighter, someone whose ego has to dominate others, this isn't going to sit well with you. This idea is to take your ego out of it and learn to be more objective. Of course you will like a candidate based on some emotional considerations, but just putting out your thoughts and listening to theirs is what creates a the ability to have a dialogue. When he preferred to vote another way on an issue, I was respectful and even shared that I could understand and might vote his way with more information. I have even been persuaded by my sons to look at issues a bit differently and they have influenced my vote. In short, their choices and thought processes were respected.

Similarly, I get their thoughts on the problem at hand that they might be having and we talk. In the end I often say, "It is your call, you have good instincts, you make the decision." We may not agree but the message is very strong that I believe in them to take responsibility and that is the rite of passage of into adulthood. "The decision is yours, the leadership on the issue is yours, and the consequences are yours" is the message I want to impart. What you bring to them in your parenting role is support if they fall or if it doesn't work out. Justin's pet sitting business didn't work out. It required a lot of work and marketing but he learned a lot about having a business. I was there to point out what went right. At times we all beat ourselves up for what goes wrong, but we also need to learn to take credit for what goes right. After all, Justin had learned how to do his business cards, how to get them out to places where he would find customers, how to do pricing, and how to research what the competition was doing. These are all great skills. Again, it is easier to be responsible for consequences if you can see a silver lining in the cloud. Like Thomas Edison, you know now how <u>not</u> to make light bulbs in a lot of creative ways after those first 1000 didn't work out.

When you do use the positive creative S.A.G.E. parenting style, you are helping your young adult to build in coping mechanisms and life skills. These last a lifetime and cut down on problems like depression and low self-esteem. They can't help but have a better quality life with skills like this and you can't help but have a better relationship with them. Instead of wanting to avoid you at all costs, you are their coach, their mentor, the type of parent they want to be. I wanted to be just the opposite sort of parent that I saw in my parents. I find it so heartwarming when Justin, Adam, and Richard talk about how they will raise their children and it is often on the principles of S.A.G.E. parenting, of delighting in the growth of their children and not turning out children who are merely labels like doctors, lawyers, business men, and business women. Be the Consultant parent that Jim Fay talks about. It is about becoming more

Chapter 5 Planting the Seeds of Success

involved in your teen or young adult's life as a consultant or a coach, not as the prison warden. I think of the sadness of my distant cousin, Thomas, who is constantly punishing and criticizing his son. In his mind, he is setting goals and setting punishments for poor outcomes. Can his son, Alex, ever set his own goals and celebrate his growth and accomplishments? Will he ever be able to do it on his own in the real world? Will he ever recover his self-esteem as a valuable and worthwhile person? Only time will tell, but I think it will be a rough road ahead because Alex has only learned that he is a failure. ✑

Chapter 6 Great Expectations

A very big problem most parents have is their expectations for teens and young adults are way off the mark of reality. If any of us are operating from a point of certain assumptions that are wrong, our solutions and approaches are going to be wrong. When I was young, part of parenting young children was to hit them for bad behavior or making mistakes. It supposedly taught them it was wrong and never to make that mistake again or suffer the consequence of physical punishment. It assumed that children were purposely choosing this behavior and I still have heard less educated parents excuse their punishments by saying the child "knew what they were doing." This parental reasoning is seen from the perspective of how we judge adult behavior. It assumes that young adults can weigh options and outcomes and have sufficient impulse control. When we believe that young adults are fully functioning adults, we are way off base. An adult who drives recklessly is choosing to do so; it isn't a matter that they don't know any better. They know how to adjust their impulses in light of options and consequences all sorted out in a matter of minutes, even seconds. But teens and young adults are still developing and learning relationship skills, life skills, and judgment skills. Their brains physiologically are still like a child's, operating from the emotional part of the brain and not from the adult physiology which is operating from the judgment part of the brain. When parents are more like the Drill Sergeant type, a challenge to their authoritarian status is seen as disrespect and a willful confrontation on the part of the young adult or teen. Often that perspective is in gross error. We need to adjust our understanding of their perspective and help them attain better behavior not just through punishment. In his constant punishment of Alex, Thomas is perhaps blurring the lines in Alex's mind as to whether he is being punished for being himself or being punished for the wrong choices. Children are quick to see punishment as personal, for being *bad*. Poor choices and wrong choices need to be seen as learning exercises. Parents go way off course in assuming that young adults get it. When I have been interviewed about why young adults returning home from college graduation just don't go out and get a job, I have responded too frequently that they don't even have the basics about job hunting, resume building, and interview skills. I've been scoffed at but where would they get these skills if they only studied and never really worked? Their brains are changing and they need these job and life skills to change their brain into a true adult brain. Parents have had these job skills so long they have forgotten that we aren't born with them.

We all know that by the teen years the body is undergoing huge shifts in hormones, creating growth and development changes that will have them start to look more like adults. Much is made of these tremendous changes and we do our best to accommodate mood swings in both males and females. But what we aren't seeing is the changes going on in their brains. In one seminar I attended, the speaker, Nancy Rahimi, a therapist, likened it to undergoing a remodel in your kitchen. If any of you have had to live through that and the frustration and upheaval of trying to carry on normal patterns of life while forcing yourself to be patient and stay focused on a positive outcome, you get a clue of what is happening. Let's look at some of these brain changes.

Sleep No More

Teens and young adults are experiencing sleep difficulties. At least two thirds of teens are experiencing what is called *phase delay.* Setting aside that we all have different biorhythms, wherein some of us prefer to get up early and go to bed early, the *lark* if you will, and others of us prefer to go to bed late and get up late, the *owls,* teens have the added problem of delayed fatigue. If most of us adults are getting tired around 10:00 at night, and ready to drift asleep at 11:00, teens will get a second wind. It is as if they drank coffee and are now wide-awake. Their sleep phase will be delayed anywhere from 1-3 hours. Add to that the fact that while most adults need about eight hours of sleep, teens need about 9½ hours, during which time they are experiencing growth hormone production. Unfortunately, our schools are designed for adults, the teachers and administrators. Teens are frequently seen as being incompliant at best, and, at worst, failures in time management for not getting enough sleep to perform during the day. This is research that has been coming out of Brown University and Stanford University for ten years! But our society seems entrenched in the *world is flat* outlook on this despite facts to the contrary. However, I did hear a report on National Public Radio recently that some schools are delaying their start times to about 9:00 a.m. to better accommodate the physiology of teens. The teachers at these schools noticed that students were more awake at the beginning of class, stayed awake through class, and performed better during class time.

I was so relieved to hear this explanation of brain development and sleep in a class two years ago. I attended a series of classes taught by Joe Connelly of the former Good Parents Inc. who specialized in helping parents to raise their teens. Joe's focus was on educating parents to be more informed about the realities of their teens and their physical, mental, and emotional growth. For the teen who has to conform to early morning high school classes and who is experiencing phase delay, he suggests getting them to go to bed at a reasonable hour and maybe reading or listening to music. This teaches them that they need some sort of wind down routine to help the body get directed toward relaxation. The body is going to still have the phase delay, but at least they might fall asleep sooner. In his coaching he helps parents understand that ultimately this is the teen's decision. This is not an ordered bedtime by a parent. It is a suggestion to help. Also, he suggests letting them take naps and sleep in on the weekends, whatever they need to catch up on deprived sleep.

My oldest son didn't suffer from this quite as bad as his younger brother. Although as a junior and senior in high school, Adam did stay out later with his friends on the weekend, he was generally up before 9:30 on weekends. Richard on the other hand was more like I was at his age. He had trouble getting to sleep before 2:00 or 3:00 a.m. even if he was quietly reading or listening to music in his room. Before I went to the Good Parents Inc. seminars, I was wondering if I should be more forceful in getting Richard to bed in the evening. I felt like a bad parent at that point. My father used to work in the car factories on the midnight shift and when I was a nurse's aide working in hospitals, I much preferred the evening or midnight shifts. I would feel nauseous

Chapter 6 Great Expectations

working the day shift for orientation. My father and I had biorhythms that were more in the line of night owls. I now can go to bed by 11:30 p.m. and get up at 7:30 a.m. and I prefer it, but it doesn't come naturally. For the growing young adult, this sleep pattern persists through the mid-20s and explains a lot about why college students prefer later classes. Again, we all attributed irresponsible attitudes and too much partying to the pattern and we were wrong. It is built into the growth phase.

Judgment Center Construction

By age 30, most adults have developed frontal lobe thinking. Or so we hope. I'm pretty sure after seeing Jerry Springer's show that for some it never happens. The frontal lobes are the part of the brain behind the forehead. This is where we are learning to reason and have good judgment. How we approach problems and figure out solutions, in part, happens in the frontal lobes. There are excellent resources out there on neurological development but I am passing on explanations given to me in parent education classes that make it more understandable. Until the teen years, much behavior is guided from the lower part of the brain known as the amygdala, which is the seat of emotions. Acquiring impulse control is a function primarily of the frontal lobes. We would like to think that merely knowing something is enough to direct behavior. It isn't. It is establishing these pathways between the emotion center and the frontal lobes, and the judgment center is critical. These are being constructed full tilt from the teen years into the mid-20s and 30s. If we look at our young adult and teen and realize that all of this construction and lying down of pathways is going on, we could be more patient and more supportive. But I find that most parents are anything but patient or supportive. As it is, teens and young adults have learned to construct *selves* to deal with the impatience, irritation, and criticism of who they are as people. Chap Clark, author *of Hurt: Inside the World of Today's Teenagers*, discusses the coping mechanisms that have created another world that these young people can live in. We frequently don't have dialogues with our teens because we aren't relating to what is really happening to them and they can't really explain it to us.

I remember one mother I counseled who was distraught when her son allegedly told friends he wanted to commit suicide. She was outraged and wondered what was it he had to complain about let alone get so depressed over. When I tried to explain that today's youths are under tremendous stress, she wasn't having any of it. Three years later, the young man came to me for counseling. A well thought out young man, mature beyond his years, he realized that his parents had wanted him to be someone else. They wanted someone who was scholarly, quiet, and polite. Who he really was, however, was someone who loved to learn hands-on, was talkative, social, introspective, and full of energy trying to learn to tone it down to be a calmer and more directed personality. It was a process and he and his father had finally come to understand one another with the father apologizing for not understanding and being too critical. We really do need to see that that they are developing that they are not full-fledged mini-adults who just need a few life experiences.

In her seminar to parents, Nancy said that neurological studies have been done on the teen brain using MRI (magnetic resonance imaging) equipment to see how the teen brain functions. As you might expect, a young child's brain has a much different functioning appearance than that of an adult. The theory was that the teen brain would be closer to the adult brain given the new adult skills that teens were acquiring along with a more adult appearance. The reality was that the teen brain more closely resembled the child brain. As I told one client, you would never yell at a toddler for failing to walk right but logically you could justify it by saying all the equipment is there. You'd be wrong of course and most of us know that. If you took that reasoning, that the equipment is there then it is their fault that they just aren't learning to walk, you would think that was barbaric parenting. We all know that the toddler will fall and take some time to master equilibrium, and time is needed for the brain to map out this new skill. The same is true with teens and young adults; they need kindness, support, and understanding as they find equilibrium in becoming adults. They will fall. This is not an opportunity to lecture and condemn; this is a time to help them find their footing and reassure them that it isn't easy. This is a time to trust in the inherent nature that they will master skills but must make mistakes along the way to mastery much as the toddler learning to walk.

"Do we coddle them?" one person asked me. The answer is yes, and no. Right now our coddling looks more like the Helicopter parent, hovering, keeping them from tasks where they might fall, fail, or get hurt. Yet in other respects, we are far from coddling, and we look like more like the unrealistic, demanding parent expecting the toddler to walk perfectly after a few short steps. This is especially the case in the areas of driving, money management, job seeking, and maintaining employment. How did we ever think that these skills just happen? In all of these areas, there are going to be errors. How we help them to negotiate and manage them is our job.

Going with the Process

We are adults and we see our lives as having evolved along a story line. Now that we can see clearly how our lives filled out, we want to have a nice, clean story line for our kids that remove some of the angst and pitfalls we experienced. It isn't going to happen. These are turbulent years of self-awareness. That is the realism we often avoid facing. They will have heartache and disappointment. When I worked in the hospital as a nurse's aide, I took care of the famous actor Gregory Peck's mother. She was recovering from a cancer surgery while he was filming the movie, *McArthur*. She was elderly and had been healthy all of her life. This was a totally devastating experience to her. A dignified and vital woman, she was without the coping skills for something this frightening. Her health had betrayed her and she didn't understand it and was somewhat depressed by it. I asked if she had ever had a serious or chronic illness before. When she said she had always been healthy, I explained to her that it was hardest for the healthy to get sick. They didn't have the coping skills others had who lived with debilitating or chronic illness. We all would love to be healthy, but those who have been ill have compassion when others are ill and must develop the capacity to live a full life with this challenge. It broadens who they are and gives them new skills.

Tony Robbins says pain is a good thing. It tells you either you need to change how you are viewing things or you need to change what you are doing. Difficulties in these adult formative years are the norm and if you show your young adult how to handle them with thoughtfulness and forgiveness, it will give them lifelong coping skills to produce a better quality life. This is going to take time. It is a process and those who

Chapter 6 Great Expectations

know me know my determined German way; I want results and I want them now! Yesterday would have been better. I very much understand linear thinking, seeing the story and visualizing the path and journey in my head only to have all these *things* mess up the glorious plans of what and where I want to go and have. Life and daily obligations seem to weigh down arrival to the goal and the vision seems so close but for daily life. Patience is something I am learning, too. Generally, when I counsel families, one or both parents are very ready for their young adult to step up into adult responsibilities. It is a shock to them when I explain the groundwork has not been done for that and we are working from square one. The good news is that it doesn't take that long.

Life is a process. To continue our gardening analogy, it is as if we are going through a garden intending to just pick apples and maybe gather some mint leaves. Suddenly we find ourselves trying to pick tomatoes, fighting with weeds, insect pests, rabbits trying to steal our food, and we get upset that all we wanted to do was gather some fruit. As soon as we think we have figured out all this gardening maintenance, we are finding the weather is causing problems; an area once shady is now in full sun, and everything shifts out of our control. We have to be resilient during this time of development if we are to teach our children to be resilient and to trust in them and trust in ourselves that it will come out all right.

I was recently at a birthday dinner for my adopted daughter, Gina. There were a dozen of us and most were work related friends including her boss and his wife, and their 16-month-old son. The parents both worked and looked worn out by their adorable toddler, who like my own sons had been and like many young children, was not able to sleep through the night yet. It was the cold and flu season so that didn't help, and work had been busy. We joked about taking a vacation and her boss said it was hard to take time off from work. He had never learned how to do that. He joked, "No one teaches you that in college!" I was also hearing on the radio that studies showed many people won't take off from work because they are sick. They persist in working only to make their co-workers sick, too. While you are going through this process an important part of it is to take time to breathe a bit and to take time to relax and let the process settle into place. We need to create a balance and let others do it too. Often, parents don't give themselves or their children permission to just take some time off. There is a lot of work going on here and part of it is to have down time. It is critical to learn when you need down time. Justin and I often went to movies. We worked hard together and we needed some recovery time in the process.

One thing I have always taught my children is to take care of themselves. It is something I want you to do too in this process. When my sons were in elementary school, we would take time off for trips to the Midwest, where most of my family lived, or to Disneyland during the school year because summer was the busiest of times for people traveling. If the boys' birthdays fell on a school day, they could take it off or save it up for a "mental day" meaning a mental health day to recoup from stress. One of my fondest memories is when my oldest son, Adam, took his birthday off in fifth grade. We took the day off to go to lunch and go shopping—his choice of activities. It was just the two of us. The world can do without us and it is good to let others see just how much you do contribute. No one values you more than when you aren't around and they have a taste of life without you!

I also let the boys take one mental day a month from school if needed. Of course, I had to explain if you were sick that month, that covered your mental day and those days did not roll over to the next month. Even Justin has learned to give himself this permission at his job. He frequently says he will be taking a mental day but doesn't. Sometimes just having the option lets you know to breathe a little and relax a bit. I myself find that if I can take a trip every three months, I come back refreshed and recharged and with a new perspective. As a Jewish rabbi pointed out to a group of us once, the only holiday in the Bible that we are commanded to celebrate is the Sabbath day. That adds up to four days a month free of work. Are you taking four days of rest off every month? We need to recharge, to learn to smell the roses. I had one girlfriend who lived out of state and I called her one-day. She felt depressed because she just couldn't get herself motivated. All she wanted to do was vegetate, sit and watch TV all day and do nothing. When I told her what the Rabbi said, I asked her when was the last time she just did nothing. She confessed that it had been months. We need to recharge and value that. I don't want you to get nervous that your young adult is just goofing off and not moving forward every day. Balance is critical for all of us. We Americans are notorious for not realizing that.

I must say that during his third year in high school, I noticed my younger son, Richard, was taking several mental days a month. My first instinct was to react like my parents and scold him for taking advantage of the gift but then I stopped. Perhaps there was a reason. Before jumping to conclusions, I needed to find out why this was happening. I asked him if he wasn't managing his time adequately, if he was overwhelmed, or if classes were giving too much homework and we had a good discussion of why this was happening. For one thing, he didn't know he was taking off more than usual. Like Tony Robbins says about pain telling you that you either need to do something different or look at it differently, he stepped back to evaluate his time management and then things went more smoothly. We must always remember that what appears to be misbehaving may be an indication to us to help recognize a problem and help solve it. Sometimes, as here, it is a matter of just pointing it out.

One of my favorite motivational speakers, Joan Borysenko, author of *Minding the Body, Mending the Mind*, says that as a speaker she travels a lot on airplanes. She knows by heart the safety drill regarding the loss of pressure in the cabin. The oxygen masks will drop down and it is important to put yours on first before helping your child or someone else. She takes this as a great metaphor for life. Take care of yourself first or you may not be able to take care of others. One of my favorite moments in coaching parents and young adults usually happens early on. We are so used to Dr. Phil and others taking a tough love approach with these problem dependent adult children. The common wisdom says the problem is them being either lazy, self indulgent, or unmotivated young adults who need a swift kick to the curb or parents who have no backbone to make their young adults get up and get on with their lives. The young adults feel bad and the parents feel like failures. When I give either party the tools and support they need, there is a moment like a sigh of relief. It is important to take care of yourself through any process. This also means finding support for your young adult, not criticism and recriminations. Processes frequently mean a lot of mistakes. That is fine. Just learn from them and do that game level again. Remember, life is a video game. You will win it and they will win if you learn from mistakes and make time to enjoy the process. ⌀

Chapter 7 Deal Breakers

No matter how well intentioned, sometimes even the best plans and hopes go without the results we want. Sometimes the relationship has suffered too much to institute an ongoing parenting plan and skills acquisition process. In times like this, you may have to remove the young adult from your home. These are extreme situations but the toxicity of what is going on will never allow any of you to reach good results. It is like expecting spoiled food to go into a recipe and come out all right. It isn't going to happen. If you can rid it of some of the decay and spoilage, it sometimes can work. Let's look at some common problems and some options. Remember, always have plan A, plan B, and if possible, plan C. But have the courage and integrity to work on each plan before abandoning it for the next.

Drugs and Other Addictions

In middle school, peers become very important to our children. That is natural and sometimes hard for parents to accept as the separation process begins in earnest. This is also the time that many young teens begin to try alcohol, tobacco, and marijuana. Some even begin to have sex. In part, these are the first steps toward adult stress management. In some regards, our culture is foolish to think that while our and previous generations used alcohol, pot, or even sex for stress relief, we can keep our children from the ill effects by simply saying, "No." When are they supposed to learn? We never address this and hope that they will sneak off and figure it out as we and previous generations did. This is unfortunate. We see increased deaths due to the new binging trends of alcohol consumption on college campuses. We do a slightly better job with sex education and easier availability of contraception choices. However, we need to have discussions with our teens and young adults about stress management and drug choices.

In Europe, families may allow their children to drink alcohol at home. It is a family matter. The legal age for public drinking and purchase is 18 years old in most countries. As a close friend from Germany said to me, "You don't teach your young to drink properly and that seems so strange." The advantage to this approach lets parents teach their children early on about social etiquette around drinking. You don't binge drink at home and so you learn your tolerance and what is and isn't acceptable behavior. When I took my sons to Europe, we already had that policy in place in our home because I had seen the European way. This trip was my graduation gift to my son, Adam, and his brother who was 15 at the time. We stayed with friends throughout England, Amsterdam, and Geneva. These families had young adult children or teens my sons' ages. It did not come as a surprise for teens around 16 and above to have a beer or glass of wine with the other adults. Richard didn't drink but Adam, at age 18, would have a glass of wine with dinner in the home of our European friends. In restaurants, Adam was able to order a glass of wine with dinner and was treated with respect. When he recently turned 21, he said it was anticlimactic after having had the responsibility to drink in public in Europe. Both of my sons had been to parties in high school where alcohol had been sneaked in and were disgusted with what they saw. They knew that they had to drive home and it was irresponsible to get drunk. As my one son said, "if I want a beer I can have it after I get home and watch TV and go to bed." They watched kids whose parents often bragged to me that their child would not drink, puke and pass out. I am not advocating that any family use the European way of approaching drinking. Still, great thought needs to be given to how we are teaching our teens and young adults to manage stress. The fact is that they will most likely drink long before they are 21. It is good to have plan A and plan B. Another life lost to binge drinking almost happened to an acquaintance of mine whose daughter had formed a club in high school that was alcohol free, but binge drank in college and had to go the hospital. The thought of losing a precious child is something none of want to hear or see. It is important that we think out how we teach our emerging adults to handle stress in a safe and healthy manner.

The bottom line here, as in taking care of oneself through the process, is learning how to manage stress. I have helped my sons and others to find ways to "manage their emotional state of mind" as Tony Robbins calls it. Tony explains that we all turn to quick fixes to handle our emotional states. Alcohol and drugs can change your *state* but so can exercise and mediation. The key is to find healthy ways to manage your emotional states so that you benefit rather than cause further harm to yourself. In his book, *The ADD Answer: How to Help Your Child Now*, Dr. Frank Lawlis, a contributor and board member to the Dr. Phil Show, explains that when treating ADD (Attention Deficit Disorder) with drugs such as Ritalin, it is critical not to expect to spend the rest of your life on these drugs. These drugs have long term, severe effects on the liver and other organs and can cause death. They ideally should be used with behavior modification and new habit formation that will naturally cause the brain to work differently. The placebo effect is a real effect. The placebo effect occurs when you give someone a medication that is harmless, like a sugar pill, but tell them that it is going to have certain effects. Believing that to be true, the patient experiences what they think is beneficial and achieves the desired outcome in many cases by believing in the sugar pill they took. The brain is a powerhouse, and again we are back to *The Secret*, and we live what we believe. This can be utilized in ADD and other emotional or psychological treatments but too often therapists rely exclusively on the drug as the magic pill. Like alcohol, the body can build up a tolerance and it becomes less effective, while the side effects can get worse. But we can modify the behavior in conjunction with the drugs as we wean the person off of the drug.

If we realize that our teens and young adults will be using drugs, alcohol, and sex as ways to change their emotional states and we have frank discussions of when it is becoming over-used and that they need to develop other ways to deal with stress, we are further ahead of the game. However, addiction does happen. Both chemical addiction and emotional addiction to these quick fixes can happen when the overuse becomes the preferred and excessive way to achieve relaxation and well-being. If this happens, nothing can be achieved in launching your young adult until the drug addiction is handled.

Chapter 7 Deal Breakers

One case that I was told about by a good friend looking for help for her friend was just such an example. Teresa was a single mother of 19-year-old John and 21-year-old Sam. Teresa was at her wits end. Both sons were living at home and expected to do household chores and make their own meals because she worked. In fact, she rather liked having them at home as long as they were contributing members of the family. John was going to community college part-time, but Sam was doing nothing constructive. For a very long time, Teresa had excused Sam's difficulties with the fact that he was diagnosed as having ADD (Attention Deficit Disorder). As I explained to the mutual friend, plenty of successful people learn to function with ADD, and in fact can be incredibly successful. Many times the ADD label is given based solely on the activeness of the child. My oldest son was very high energy, as am I. I learned to channel his energy with lots of play dates to the playground and active sports like swimming and soccer. In an episode of the TV show *Super Nanny*, Jo the nanny was confronted by parents of an extremely active child that the parents felt must suffer from Attention Deficit Hyperactive Disorder (ADHD). Jo was able to reassure them that the child just needed to get involved in some constructive play that burned off energy. Too often we want to label and medicate when there are perfectly normal solutions that don't involve drugs and that save the child from living the life of a label. Nothing is worse than becoming a label and being excused from real life. Justin, my *adopted* son, had real learning disabilities. But I told him everyone has something they need to learn with or deal with and figure out ways to work around or compensate for. We all have strengths and we all have weaknesses. We need to maximize the strengths and work around the weaknesses.

But for Teresa, Sam was a label and couldn't be expected to function like the rest of us. Sam began to feel like a loser. My response was that Sam needed a job if he wasn't going to college or receiving skills training. At one point, Teresa threw Sam out of the house and he lived on the streets until she felt guilty and let him return. Already on Ritalin, which is a type of speed, a stimulant, and easily addictive, Sam spent his time partying and selling drugs to provide for his partying. It never occurred to anyone that it was odd that he was able to be selling drugs but couldn't find a legitimate sales job. When told to go work or school, he lamented that he was a failure and just couldn't succeed. Despite being very handy repairing cars as a hobby, he had never gotten his driver's license and declined Teresa's offers to send him to auto mechanics training. As his behavior became more disruptive in the household, I suggested that since Teresa did not have the courage to be disciplined and consistent in her rules and requirements with Sam, that she buy him a one way ticket to go live with his father out of state. The hope was that given a stronger hand and a good male role model, Sam would grow up and assume adult responsibilities. Unfortunately, unbeknownst to anyone, dad had a crack habit and Sam spent a lost year with dad.

As things fell apart with dad, Sam went to live with an aunt for six months, and then returned home, promising to turn over a new leaf. I counseled that before he entered the house, there should be a game plan of what he was to do and accomplish and an exit strategy if he failed. Teresa didn't want to take the time to work this out. Although he was much more appreciative of his mother and the life she provided, he still had nothing to contribute to the household. He reverted back to his old habit of doing what he wanted. I relayed to our mutual friend that now we were fairly sure that Sam was an addict and nothing could move forward until Sam went to rehab. After several run ins with the law, Teresa put Sam into a 45 daylong rehab. Sam ran away after two weeks but returned to it and admitted that his life was a mess and if it was going to change, he needed to make some changes. Alcohol and drug addicts can't be reasoned with. They aren't normal people when using. They are living, walking drug consumers and nothing else in life matters.

If you have a young adult who is incapacitated by drugs, you must have an intervention and get them to rehab. They present a toxic and sometimes dangerous environment to you and your family. Furthermore, you enable them even without meaning to do so. Sam went into long term detox and rehab. At long last he was made to be responsible and he started to feel better about his life and found hope. Hopefully, Teresa will make a game plan before he returns to live with her. This is the opportunity to get plan A, plan B, and plan C in place. Having no plans is a set up for problems. What would I counsel? She has to hand hold him through getting his driver's license. She literally needs to set dates and take him there for his permit. It should only take a few months for him to pass the driving test. He has driven without a license, which is a bad and risky choice. At the same time, she should have him either ready to get employment or go to the trade school in auto repair. If he is indecisive, then she should send him. With job training, he will be able to start a job and make money. She cannot let him sit around and be left to make decisions. He likes the structure of rehab. She should replicate that. He should be moved out in less than a year and she can help him find a place. However, it seemed she liked having her sons live at home. There is nothing wrong with that but then she should require him to pay rent. It is critical that he learn to manage money, since rent and mortgages are a big part of managing life. She should consider that, given her own personality, it will be too easy for him to lose employment and/or not pay the bills he needs to learn to pay. Money management skills are the hardest to acquire when young adults are still living at home. It can be done but it needs structure. What she doesn't want is for him to fall back into his party at home ways. Any income should go toward bills and life's necessities. If he returns to drugs, he needs to be gone. Either pay two months' rent on a place and let him manage after that or negotiate partial payment for a while of a room or apartment. Old habits easily return when you return to the familiar settings that they flourished in. My recommendation would be for him to live on his own for a few years for his own good. Addictions are very easy to return to and you want to maximize success. One statistic I was told by a professional interventionist is that in short-term treatment, around 30 days, the success rate is 2-10 percent. In long term programs of around 90 days, the success rate is higher at 25 percent. The benefit of the longer program is that it teaches the addict to live life sober and keeps them out of the environment and away from the enablers that helped form the addictive life. As much as Teresa wanted her sons living at home, there are times we have to put the best interests of our young adult child first.

This is hard for parents. I had other parents who were dealing with an ADD son. The stepfather and mother had gotten together when the young man was in his mid-teens. Having been a single mother of three, the family had toxic and abusive relationships with one another during her welfare years and her drug recovery years. Sean, the stepfather, was doing all he could to be a good role model and help Fred stay on his ADD medicine and get through high school. It became evident that the friends that Sean had were doing drugs. Sean hoped that he could still turn things around. Several years went by and Fred never found time to get a job. When I counseled that Sean needed to literally go with Fred to get a job or the descent into drug addiction would

Chapter 7 Deal Breakers

get worse, Sean seemed confident that a little more patience and love would rule the day.

Fred was kicked out of high school in the first few weeks of his senior year for a prank. Sitting behind another student, he leaned over and tried to ignite the young man's shirt. The shirt was synthetic, melted, and caused a small burn on the student's back. Fred had no desire to get his GED, go to work, or do anything other than party. At this point, Fred needed to go to rehab but his mother, who felt guilty for his neglected and harsh early years of life, didn't agree. Time was running out since at age 18 you can't place your child into detox; they legally get to make their own decisions from that age on. Having made his own decisions and running wild for years, Fred would not be coerced into detox as easily as our friend from the previous story, Sam. When very unsavory characters started coming around and the physical abuse of his siblings started, Sean had to toss his stepson out of the house. Fred went to live with his grandmother for a while but his late nights and obvious drugged or drunken states at all and any time of the day led grandma to kick him out of her house. Fred was homeless unless he made friends with someone and managed a few weeks or days on their sofa. He was in and out of jail and continued a life none of us want. Without detox, Fred would become one of the homeless bums we see in the big cities. But Fred's stepfather didn't give up. Fred was not allowed to live at home but eventually he did get help. He looked me up one day and I was stunned. He had a job, he was polite, nicely dressed, and had a girlfriend. He was a fine example of young man starting his life. Most importantly he was away from drugs.

Make no mistake, the time to get some rehab skills and awareness even with the probability of relapse is before your children hit 18 years old. But if you can talk them into it at later times, that is good, too. The bottom line is that the chances are slim of a meaningful life as long as they pursue drug or alcohol addiction to all else. I talk all the time about getting teens to have jobs in high school. I've seen too often that bored teens easily fall into the party scene. It is too frequent that working parents don't know what is going on. You may wish that your teen is studying hard and trying to get into that fine college where the mysterious high paying jobs are just waiting, but too often they are not. When teens have to manage school and work, it gives them a sense of adult responsibilities and money management. Money is a great motivator for young employees. Teens and young adults have more focus in their lives when working and less need to overdo the party aspect.

In some cases, teens use sex as an emotional buffer to life's stress, much as others use drugs. It happens with adults too. When stress happens we try to find ways to feel better, to change our emotional states. With raging hormones, it is too easy for this to be an outlet in some cases. It seems to be like a drug when there is promiscuity but sex and an intimate relationship can cause more issues for parenting. We still have to move our young adults to independence. There are still life skills and job skills that need to be acquired but the dynamics are different.

I notice many teens don't enter into these intense emotional relationships. Some date or have the occasional boyfriend or girlfriend but teens often find these to be demanding relationships and aren't quite ready to take on the emotional care of another. The good news is that it can become a motivator for the young adult to become independent. Even though these relationships may persist for a year or longer, they are fraught with a lot of tension. I have watched both scenarios. On the one hand are the relationships where the love interest is a welcome part of the family and on the other hand are the parents with an intense desire to break the couple apart. What I try to encourage in parents is to understand if your teen or young adult is involved romantically, be compassionate and know that this too is another set of life skills. Navigating romance and having your emotional needs met and meeting another's emotional needs is very complex. It is hard for some parents to realize that their child will be turning to this person for a great deal of emotional support through this relationship. Be respectful of this relationship unless it is abusive.

Where this starts to impact the game plan for adult independence is how the two lovebirds are deciding dependence and independence of self with their partners. When I give talks to parent groups, I tell them you are raising your child to be dependent or independent. Once the path is set for dependence, you have a problem human being. They are learning that they have a job in life and that is to find someone to take care of them and their responsibilities. We all know them. As fully-grown adults, they are lazy, usually ungrateful, draining, demanding, and hurtful. They are like emotional parasites. They have learned to live life this way. I get consultations for adults well on their way to this life style in their 30's and 40's. At that point, the way to handle them is very different because they don't want to change, and after years of being this way, it works well for them. Usually a family member asks me how I can change them so that they aren't so draining and dependent. The answer is you can't. You have to stop enabling them and limit their contact. But that is my second book. Having been a highly independent person most of my life, I have found that the dependent personalities gravitate to me like bees to honey. I have counseled both parents and young adults who are independent but find themselves with the dependent partner. This is hard because the young adult generally hasn't had a lot of dating experience and worries about ever finding a partner to love them again. They worry whether or not they should learn to put up with situations where they do more giving than taking. When you have dated a while, you learn what will work in a relationship and what is a deal breaker. But teens and young people don't have this perspective yet. As with finding a job, finding a mate needs a skill set.

I remember when my first real boyfriend broke up with me in college; I was devastated. It seemed that I had waited all my teen life for someone, and who knew if it would ever happen again? My mother sat silent with me on the sofa in the living room as I cried and poured out my fears. She had no answers. That scared me. Perhaps my fears were right! They weren't, but this points out the confusion of our role in these situations. What is our role when our teens and young adults are going through these relationship trials and tribulations? It is to nurture and comfort. It is not to take sides. I see it as a chance to debrief on the one hand and help the young adult devise care giving strategies for recovery from the break up.

Your child is having a broken heart. A broken heart like a broken limb has to heal. Reassure your teen or young adult that these things happen. It is part of growing up. Their job is to decide if there could have been better ways of handling the situations that caused the break up or if they fell in love with one person only to find that they changed into another in day-to-day life. Too frequently, we fall for the Mask. All of us do and have done that. The Mask is who the person is during courtship. We all are encouraged to put our best foot forward when we enter a new relationship. I learned a

Chapter 7 Deal Breakers

rule of thumb very late in life. The rule was, wait six months and then ask yourself if this is the person you want to be in a relationship with. After about six months, those who are really good at creating the Mask generally can't sustain it. I'm not saying everyone has this deceptive Mask or that it is far off from who they really are. Some people don't bother creating much of a mask, so what you see pretty much is what you get. Others have a definite courtship mask that is very different from who they are down the line. Generally, the best Mask makers are kind, giving, generous, and courteous and then down the line few of those characteristics are present in sufficient quantities to maintain a romance or serious relationship. It feels like the old bait and switch. Too often, many of us continue to hope that we can earn back the person we fell in love with when we fell for the Mask, not the real person. When I counsel young people and even friends, I point out that if the person never goes back to being who they fell in love with, would this be all right?

I have had two friends that this happened to. For Tina, it was important to decide if she wanted to marry Bart. An older and established man, his being attentive to her needs changed into inflexible control of her and their activities after a period of time. Like many of us, she thought the issues would be resolved with marital counseling and then they could plan their wedding. After numerous meetings with a therapist, things didn't seem much improved. Finally, the therapist met one on one with each of them. He was direct with Tina and asked, "If Bart never changed would it be all right?" Tina was horrified. Of course not! The therapist then said, well in Bart's mind he was perfectly fine, she was the one who needed to change and all would be well. She realized that if that was who he was, she would never be happy, so she left. When MaryAnn from our earlier discussion found out that eight years after her divorce, her ex-husband was remarrying, she was devastated. Her ex had been seeing his fiancé for over five years and MaryAnn thought it would never come to this. In her mind, she still cherished the dream that she and her ex could *evolve*, that maybe who she fell in love with would return. I told her she fell in love with the Mask, not the person. There was no evolving because it wasn't real. This is very common. We fall for the Mask and need to realize to evaluate who the person really is. If your young adult is sounding like they may have fallen for the Mask and want a return to the early days of courtship and who their partner was then, you have to be gentle in letting them know that this is a big life lesson. Generally, that Mask is who our heart desires and it takes time to get over the fact that who was wearing it for the moment wasn't the same as the Mask.

Another difficult situation is when your young adult is in a relationship where there is an imbalance of give and take. This is another relationship issue that comes up frequently. I have seen situations of independent young men with the dependent *damsel* in *distress* or *princess* personality. Sometimes these young women proudly flaunt their "high maintenance" status as if that makes them more valuable. Actually, when you hear "high maintenance", think self absorbed and self-centered. Whatever you give of yourself and gifts will be weighed and harshly judged by their demands for perfection. If you don't value yourself, this will work. Conversely, I have seen women who are maidservants to their demanding male partners. These men too are high maintenance and the belief that you can give more, do more, and be more is erroneous. You will never meet their standard.

In both of these circumstances, a way to help your teen or young adult is to evaluate that quality of their relationship through a scale my own life coach taught me. On a percentage scale from 0 percent to 100 percent, how much are you giving to the relationship compared to your partner? Dr. Phil always says that relationships aren't 50/50 but 100/100 percent and this is true for the best and strongest relationships. A high maintenance person will have a much-distorted view of what they are giving. Their mere presence gracing another's life in their mind puts them way over the 50 percent mark. It may even be as high as 80 percent. In reality, their giving is about what they want to give, not what the other person wants to receive. Generally, they give what costs little to them without feeling put out. Most of the high maintenance people I have seen tend to give about 10-20 percent at best. This means that their partner is giving 80-90 percent and this takes a toll on the self-esteem of the giver. Their high maintenance partner frequently keeps the giver off balance by judging the quality of what was given or done. This deflects the attention from the fact that they are not giving much or are not being appreciative enough.

If you are asking what this has to do with independence and launching your teen or young adult, this scale has a lot to do with helping them to understand interpersonal dynamics. The scale can be used in all types of relationships, not just romantic ones. In friendships, at jobs, and in family relationships, it is important to know how much you are giving and what you are being required to give on an interpersonal level. This also goes back to boundaries, and as Dr. Phil says, "You teach people how to treat you." My life coach, Lorri, says that when she uses the scale, she then assigns a letter to them just like grades in school. For example, if you are giving 90-100 percent, that is an "F" relationship. Conversely, that means you are getting only ten percent not including the overpriced value of their mere presence. If you are giving 70-90 percent then maybe that is "C" or "D" grade relationship. We all have different tolerance levels so maybe what is barely above failing for one, may be average for another. But in an average relationship, you may find demands on your time and energy and focus on the other with very little emotional sustenance. In the work world, we endure this quite a bit. Sometimes, even in our family. We do this because there is extra pay off. In a job, you have income security so you will put up with more. In families, there is the security of help during times of crisis. But the quality relationships, the ones where you give 60-70 percent conversely receiving 30-40 percent are on the grade level of around a "B". At the "A" level, we feel like we are getting as much as we give and usually we are getting a lot of emotional reward. You can see that using those magic words of "please", "thank you", and for those difficult moments, "I'm sorry" can boost up the grade of your relationship. To have balance in your life, it is good to have very few "D" relationships, a few "C" relationships and then the rest in the "B" or "A" area. Most of us have way too many of the "C" and below with only one or two about the "C" level. It is important to realize that relationships can bounce back and forth in their grades. We all can go up and down in grading, depending on the various stages and episodes in our life. What I notice with many people is that when you let too many "C" and "D" relationships in your life, you start to starve for emotional sustenance and your self-esteem goes down. People with this lower self-esteem feel they deserve these relationships when what they need to do is wean them out of their lives and look for better grade relationships.

When you share these observations either as the relationship is ongoing or if it has come to an end, be generous in spirit. These are hard life lessons. I know several parents not happy with their young adult's choice of a romantic partner. I have talked with one young man, Charles, who has a very dependent girlfriend. She never got her

Chapter 7 Deal Breakers

driver's license so he must drive her places and run the necessary errands. She also likes to be with him constantly when they aren't working or going to classes. Her parents are going through a divorce and she leans on him heavily for emotional support and sometimes financial support. He relished playing the knight in shining armor but eventually, you want to take the armor off and it is starting to drain him. Like so many others, he thinks in time, it will be different that she will reciprocate and do the same for him. What I have told one young woman also waiting for things to change is that just because there is the ability to change, doesn't mean it will happen. Often the dependent, draining person doesn't believe his or her partner's threats of ending things if things don't change to be more equal in giving. Sometimes the dependent one goes on to the next relationship after the break up and is more independent or has learned a lesson, but most of the time, things don't change. Once you have said your peace, be kind. One mother related to me that she tried to make friends with her son's girlfriend only to be rebuffed. She offered to take her out to lunch or to go shopping only to be politely declined. Now her biggest worry is that he will try to choose his college based on staying close to his girlfriend. It does happen and isn't the end of the world. There is always time to transfer should the relationship change. It is important to remember, this relationship, like getting a job, is about acquiring life and interpersonal skills.

When you are giving your teen or young adult advice, keep the tone neutral and don't condescend. It is best to provide this from the perspective of what you think works well. It is much easier to hear someone's opinion or approach instead of being told how to view things. No one enjoys that level of disrespect. But as you get them to understand relationship experience and evaluation as to what is or isn't working for them, give them credit for what they have discovered and how they have handled it. Always find ways to point out how they are doing well. When I was talking to Charles about his very dependent girlfriend, I did point out that he was a good guy in his helping her and even trying to help her parents diffuse the arguing during the divorce. We all need to know what we are doing right in a situation. At times of stress and confusion, we need to look at our successes and sometimes we just can't see them through all that is going on. When I was a student at the University of Washington in Seattle, I remember seeing a comic posted on the door of one of the teaching fellow's offices for a biology class I was taking. Under the photo of a guy in the swamps with water up to his waist, it read, "It is difficult to remember why you came to drain the swamps when you are up to your ass in alligators." Life is frequently like that for many of us. Most of us aren't busy patting ourselves on the back for our minor successes because our primary focus on all the alligators swimming around us. That kindness of a pat on the back lets us know we are making progress and that maybe our instincts and talents are getting us through the maze. You still have to be their coach of inspiration as well as their soft place to fall.

This brings us to the other piece of navigating relationships and that is helping them take care of themselves through stressful, emotional times like a break up. Nothing rocks your core of who you are and your self-worth like a break up. As with our previous conversation on learning to deal with stress, it is even more critical here. I wish my mother would have told me first of all, that breaking up is normal and I will heal. To a young person, it feels like the pain will remain forever. Recently, my adoptive son, Justin, went through a bit of heartache. He was trying online dating since several months of crushes weren't netting any love interests. It always feels like everyone else finds love but you, however everyone experiences not getting the one they want and not finding someone to be interested in at the moment. After meeting one girl for coffee, he discovered that she wasn't as she portrayed herself and wasn't really interested in a long-term romance. Another lady insulted his looks saying, "Why would anyone want to date you?" One way he lets off steam is to go to the gym. At the gym, he ran into three girls he had crushes on over the past year and they basically ignored him. It was too much. I'm glad that he didn't go out and get drunk as many of my favorite country western songs talk about. We sat down for a glass of wine and I explained that this is the nature of dating. It is about finding out who is a good match and who isn't and they are doing the same. It takes time. We talked about how he falls *in love* a bit too quickly and maybe it was the Mask he was falling for, how they looked and moved and that initial infatuation which hooks you. I explained we all do that and you learn not to put your heart out there too quickly for a bruising. I said just as bad as putting it out too quickly is not putting it out at all for fear of getting hurt. It is like everything else, about balance. One of the girls he had a crush on he couldn't even imagine why he had felt that way anymore. I told him it was good that he was seeing that you do heal when these things don't work out and perhaps he'll assess a partner a bit better in the future. It is like buying a new car. After driving a few, you get good at evaluating what appeals to you and what doesn't. It doesn't take a lot of thinking and weighing aspects anymore; you zoom in on things quickly and address them more quickly. Like all the other skills that are being worked on, even dating has a learning curve. We made a plan for him over the next few days to take care of himself in his bruised heart condition. He would go to the movies with friends, maybe get a massage, do things that relaxed him and made him feel better. Once he told friends of his sad state, everyone was rallying around him sending their love and support. This is this kind of life skill you want to bring to your young adult. How does this relate to getting launched into adulthood? It brings a sense of problem solving and balance to a very important aspect of life. It gives them an inner core of strength and confidence that they can meet these curve balls that life throws at us. As always this is a process and romantic relationships take years to figure out. It is really hard to stand by and watch a dependent personality use and perhaps emotionally abuse our children when we know they deserve better. There are always two sides to a story. Don't be too quick to judge. You can acknowledge that they may be hurt but it is their choice how they want to proceed in the relationship. For one client, I once asked, "Is this an A or B quality relationship and if it isn't, is this how you want to spend your life?" The final answer is theirs.

What you want to do is emphasize the ability of your teen to acquire independence on their own and not have them look to other people for financial support and enabled dependence. Young relationships seldom last. We must remember that the young adult brain is still growing and there are new choices and preferences happening frequently. If you can enlist the support of your young adult's partner, so much the better, but the most powerful focus is you on your child and trust that they can build their independence. I've been divorced twice. I've watched some of my friends in their early 20's and 30's lose their love partner to car accidents and fatal illness as well as through divorce. There is no total security in a relationship or in life, be that a job, a career, or a partner.

I have seen young adults move back home after a break up. I suspect there is some need for comfort and support. There is nothing wrong with that but do not let them

Chapter 7 Deal Breakers

back in until you have an agreement of how they will heal and get back out on their own. As I have told many young people, a broken heart is like a pulled muscle. It takes months to heal. If you broke a leg or pulled a muscle in your back, the doctor would tell you how you need to take it easy and give you prescriptions for medicine and when to exercise again. The same is true of a broken heart. If you can remodel your life like one young woman, Lisa did after her break up did, and it helps enormously. It gives the feeling of moving on and no longer being the naïve person who was hurt.

Lisa had boyfriends before but her relationship with John was in college, a time when most young people are feeling more adult. They are learning to manage their day-to-day living and relying more on friends and peers. She and John both came from divorced homes with absentee fathers and shared a lot of interests in common. They had the same major, many of the same classes, the same groups of friends, and were in the same activities. He was the first serious boyfriend to break up with her and she took it hard. After weeks of depression and lack of sleep, I suggested she take charge of her life, do what she loved to do. Lisa needed to be empowered. She needed clearer boundaries with John who continued to walk her to classes and call her. It hurt. The more she stood up for herself the better she felt. She began to look into the dream of transferring to a college she had wanted to get into as a freshman. Lisa got into the college and made plans to move across the country and enter the college of her dreams. Suddenly, she felt empowered and wiser. There was the added benefit that she no longer saw the same places and faces to remind her of the memories leading up to the breakup. You can stay where you are and take up new hobbies, join a gym or a different gym, and do things to give yourself new memories that are not contaminated by the old ones. Learning to heal after an emotional injury is an important life skill. If your young adult is returning home for any reason, make sure that you both have agreed to how long the healing process will be and what their goals are for a new life. This gives two messages. One is that you know they will heal and you have faith in them dealing with this situation while providing support. Second is the message that yes, they will heal and this is an opportunity to write a new life for themselves that it is an adventure. This is an opportunity, not just a disaster. Adventures give us an adrenalin rush. It makes you feel better and develop hope and excitement. You want to replace the feelings of loss and depression with those more positive feelings. In most cases with a new game plan and new choices, people can recover enough within six months to get back out on their own. Somewhere within that first year, they should be ready to re-enter adult life.

Whether it is a break up or some other emotional trial that shakes up your young adult, coming home should be a brief respite, not a lifelong goal. In one case where I was consulted briefly, Elizabeth was worried about her son, Peter. Peter had gone to good private schools and was expected to go on to college as is the dream of many parents. A semester at the local community college left Peter turned off to college and lost. Since Elizabeth was divorced from Peter's dad and Peter was still living at home with his very indulgent father, she was at a loss as to how to motivate her son to get out on his own. By his mid-20s, with many of his friends off living on their own, Peter decided to go to a big city about 100 miles away from his home town. He would live in an apartment with his cousin and his cousin, having been on his own and established, would help Peter find a job. With no previous job experience, Peter got a job in a car repair shop as an office clerk. When the boss sent him out with money to get some items for the shop and buy the boss some lunch, Peter used the money to also buy himself some lunch. He had no sense that he was supposed to provide for lunch for himself with his own money and didn't understand that his boss was not like his father who gave him anything he wanted. Needless to say when the receipts didn't tally with the returned change, Peter was fired. This was the first time Peter had to be responsible in an adult capacity for his mistakes and it scared him. He had no skill set for this. To make matters worse, within the following week while job hunting, Peter left food on the stove cooking in the apartment while he was gone. He had become distracted and totally forgotten about it. It caught fire and the fire department had to come. While there was smoke damage and some fire damage, the apartment building did not suffer major repair costs. However, he was kicked out of his apartment. He went home to daddy. This is a young man without life skills and without resilience. Once at home, he was idle and without a job for long stretches while dad provided for him. He no longer saw himself as able to care for himself and, now in his mid-30s, he is still at home. He has a low paying job as a security guard without goals for any sort of career or future. This was a talented young man who could have learned a trade or got an art degree and become very successful. At his age now, he is beaten down by life. Things could change except that his father doesn't like being alone and prefers to enable this dependent state. Should parents let their young adults come home to save money for a house or to recover? Yes, but not to cripple them into being your companion. Elizabeth said her son always wanted to have a family of his own. Yet without life skills and the help he needs to grow up, Peter will be a lonely old man in his father's house and not have any of his life's dreams if this continues.

In short, some things may drive your young adult back home or add to problems of getting them launched. Drugs are a deal breaker and so are any relationships that cripple and make your young adult dependent. At least with the latter, you can work around them. But if you get resistance, you need to treat that the same as a drug problem. The young adult must leave. If you become an enabler of their failure to launch, you are not helping them or yourself.

Abuse and Abusive Relationships

One of the most helpful therapies I participated in while I was in my 20s was group therapy using transactional analysis. It was a concept developed in the 1970's by Eric Berne. As used in the group therapy that I was in, the focus was on the dysfunctional triad in a relationship. Many of us in the group were still dealing with the unhealthy family dynamics that we grew up in and wanted to rid our lives of their destructive influences. I'm sure that the theories have evolved but the simplicity of the model explained to us was easy to understand and work with to effect change. For much of my coaching, I use different helpful models of behavior. They all have their critics and their fans. I only put them out there because if we can begin to understand one another in a way that is useful, it will help us to be calmer in our dealings and less judgmental. I like simplicity and I like when you have a model that lets you see patterns and help you to better understand how to deal with those patterns.

The basic premise of transactional analysis as explained to me was that we all have emotional needs that we need satisfied. If those needs aren't satisfied in a healthy way, an unhealthy triad of roles will emerge to get the needs met. Visualize an equal sided

Chapter 7 Deal Breakers

triangle. Each leg of the triangle has a label. One is the *Victim,* the other is the *Persecutor,* and the third is the *Rescuer.* The labels are pretty self-explanatory. Persecutors harass and attack others verbally and emotionally. They can go further and become physically abusive. They dominate and control others by the bully mentality. They are dictators and they want all the power. Victim is a role of never having power. The world acts on you and you take it. You don't fight back and you do whatever your Persecutor demands. You can readily see that children often have this role. In terms of boundaries, you never get to have any and self-esteem couldn't be any lower. Rescuer is a role that has some power for coming to the aid of another. This is the proverbial knight in shining armor whether male or female. Rescuers like to see themselves as helpful and caring. I know because I have been one. However, we are talking about a dysfunctional state and as such they are more apt to be enablers of dysfunction. Assisting in perpetuating dysfunction is not a good thing. That is how Rescuers can recover. By realizing that they are helping Persecutors or Victims to continue their unhealthy path, a Rescuer can find a more balanced role in which to enjoy being compassionate and caring.

Generally, we have a favorite or preferred role if we are living in this emotional triangle, but because a lot of it revolves around ego strength and the need for power to support that ego need, we may vacillate between two favorites. However, all of us will use all of them over a lifetime of dysfunctional relationships. I suddenly saw the dynamics between my parents and myself in a new light. In fact, I saw a lot of my relationships in a new light. It becomes interesting to watch other relationships around you whether at work or with family members and their families and see what roles people prefer. It is sad to say, but most of us live in dysfunction that brings this triangle to life. It is part of what was passed down to us long ago through the many generations. The idea is to leave behind these roles and to become more balanced and honest in how we get our emotional needs met.

Both of my parents were big on being Persecutors as was the model for parents for centuries. "Spare the rod, spoil the child" was a common adage as was "children should be seen and not heard." In many countries for most of humanity, the father owned the wife and children as property. There couldn't be a better set up for the Persecutor role. My parents made sure to point out the mistakes and shortcomings of us kids in venomous tirades. I'm sure it had been no different than when they were children. It was perfectly acceptable to name call and denigrate your child. With the most severe Persecutors, you can never please them; you can never be enough or do enough for them to cease their criticism. This was a shock to me because I always thought that things could be solved by doing more, performing more, performing more correctly and that would win their approval but it never did. It helped to drive me into severe depression and attempted suicide. While Persecutors like to tell themselves that they are only being *helpful* what they really are doing is deflecting attention away from their own shortcomings and making themselves feel superior by tearing down someone else. My father was especially good at this. Persecutors often become bullies and abusers. They love the rush of power over another, determining their happiness by dishing out criticism and withholding praise. They are the "right fighters" that Dr. Phil describes on his show. They have to have the last word and will argue everything to prove they are right and you are wrong. The dysfunction here is that they can never get the love and respect they crave so badly when they damage and destroy the very people from whom they want it. They do get attention but they leave the interaction feeling empty, or at best they are the winner of the "you are worse than me" contest. Persecutors are very angry people, and as we discussed, anger is either fear, hurt, or frustration. In my experience with Persecutors, they tend to be extremely afraid and extremely hurt. Acting out in this role is how they manage the anxiety associated with those feelings.

My father's second preferred role was as the Victim. Let me say here that this is from my perspective and my interactions with my father. These are the patterns I noticed and my other siblings may have seen things differently. We act differently with different people. These are dynamics and dynamics change depending on a lot of factors. I want you to try to see patterns that you can work with and I am using my life as an example. My father had moments of being kind and funny and supportive, but for me, they were few and far between. That was not true for some of my other siblings and yet was the same for others. The point is to look at the relationships in your life and with your teens and young adults and reflect on the patterns in the interactions. At the end of life, you will remember the predominate patterns. Those more than anything define you and how you are viewed by others. If you are balanced and out of this dysfunctional pattern, you will have a warm loving family like we all want.

But as I was saying about my father's second pattern of being a Victim, I have noticed that the Victim role is what bullies will turn to when the person they are trying to persecute turns on them. I was a Victim as my second favorite role. I obviously couldn't be a Persecutor as both my parents had that one covered in abundance. The advantage to being a Victim is you aren't responsible for your actions. You walk around attracting Rescuers and it leaves you powerless except to the point of manipulating your Rescuer to care for you. However, you don't have the power we all need for a healthy ego. There is also the problem of finding a Rescuer because they don't show up on cue. In a family they can be more easily identified. Sometimes being the Victim is a way to placate the Persecutor. Victims don't develop good life skills and mastery of living and selecting their choices. They can't have dreams because that is a place of self-empowerment. They draw a universe of *bad luck* and their greatest joy gets to be a pity party. Physical abusers are very good at being both the Persecutor and the Rescuer. Their victim is kept in check with physical, emotional, and verbal abuse. But then they dole out the good times and the good attention so there is *hope* for more of the latter and a reduction in the former. This is not to say my father was physically abusive other than what was common at the time in terms of beating us with the belt. But his Persecutor role was bad enough and the predominate pattern for him as I experienced and remembered him. In the Victim role my father never wanted to take responsibility for his mistakes; he had excuses and he was a victim to them. While women can be damsels in distress just like in the fairy tales, waiting to be rescued by the handsome prince, for men, a victim role is not a masculine position. It has to eat away at their standing as men.

My favorite role was the Rescuer. It has the feel of integrity, of being a good person, and even if you are a victim at other times, you can still give more and sacrifice more for another in rescuing them from life's downfalls. It lets you be a hero, in your mind at least. My mother was big on a Persecutor first and a Rescuer second. The problem with being a Rescuer is that it can very quickly become an enabler and a doormat. I attracted Victims like crazy who wanted to sit back and let me make their lives work. I wondered why they never seemed to get out of their dire circumstances and why bad

Chapter 7 Deal Breakers

luck trailed them like a shadow. It also made me into a doormat all the while thinking I was being compassionate and helpful year in and year out. Since taking Tony Robbins classes, I have learned to respect my own self worth and stop helping those who are determined to be Victims and stop enabling that life attitude on their behalf. As my own life coach said to me once, "Ellen, do you really think that it serves your higher self and theirs to keep them where they are through enabling them?" It doesn't, but too many enablers are victims to their own cowardice to stand up and refuse to enable. Until and unless they get that they are being the devil's workers in enabling others to stay victims and not realize their full potentials, they will continue to harm themselves in the role of enabler as well as harm the very people they want to help. People don't change until we change. That is true for marriage and it is true for parent-child relationships. I want you to look at whether or not there is a pattern with your teen or young adult in which you are the Rescuer, enabling them to stay a victim to not growing up. It isn't healthy for either of you.

Some form of the transactional analysis triangle and role play surfaces in most relationships. The trick is always balance. Finding how to be compassionate without enabling is a balancing act. The healthy way to do that is learning to be supportive, not enabling. It is important to voice alternatives or point out potential problems supplemented with statements of praise, which is more preferable than being critical and judgmental. The former approach will always be heard while the latter approach will go in one ear and out the other, causing damage to the relationship in the transit. If you or your young adult tends towards being a Victim, it is more rewarding to challenge yourself and to recognize ways to overcome limitations and obstacles and give yourself praise for baby steps. These are healthy life management skills. Becoming the Consultants to our adult children as opposed to the Drill Sergeant or Helicopter parent is a much better role to create. This will also eliminate the dysfunctional triangle of Victim, Persecutor, and Rescuer. If you can picture yourself as a coach to a player on a team or as a gardener or a builder of a home, that vision will give you a better and more constructive role.

You are trying to create an outcome with your young adult. The healthier outcomes for your emotional needs will flow from taking on the job and role. One time Justin was recounting to me how frustrated he was at work. His boss had criticized him for not doing something when in fact he had never been assigned the task. He took it personally as most of us would. I noticed this happened before and was a pattern. His upset, hurt, and anger then transferred to other workers. His boss was indeed trying to pass the blame for a task not getting assigned and did this often. Clearly, the boss wasn't good at managing tasks and workloads and assigning them to get done. I told Justin that being emotional is not a solution. The solution is to take on a role like an actor. We picked a favorite hero of his to use as his visual. He was to assume that calm demeanor and point out that he always fulfilled his assigned tasks and he couldn't be held responsible for his boss's failures in assignment. If possible, he could offer concern to the boss that there is so much to do and it is hard to remember everything that needs to be done and assigned. Justin would be glad to help his boss develop some method for clear daily assignments in writing so that the boss could check to make sure he hadn't forgotten something. Be clear, be calm, and don't get into a fight. The first time he tried this approach his boss was stunned and tried to intimidate Justin. However, Justin remained calm and offered understanding and compassion but refused to take the blame. After that things worked out just fine between them. If you can role play your way into handling situations, it soon becomes a part of who you are and creates that balance.

I work with clients to get them out of the dysfunctional roles of Victim, Persecutor, and Rescuer. If I can get them out of these and turn them into healthier roles, we stand the best chance of the young adult following suit. Remember, their brains are still growing and trying to learn to function from the judgment center to control the emotion center. It is best when everyone can stay out of the emotion center and focus on creating a life result that also creates good judgment. That does not mean you can't make mistakes. Anything not turning out as expected or desired is a learning opportunity. You'll be surprised at how calm you become after a while going with the situation and learning from it. ✍

Chapter 8 Boundaries and Bubbles

No, I have not mixed this up with a book on fairy tales. I have found there are two ways of understanding yourself and protecting yourself in a broad way that you can teach to your teens and young adults that will give them flexibility and adaptability for many if not most situations. Boundaries will help you defend and protect yourself, and all too frequently we don't have clear boundaries. Bubbles are how we grow. If we see ourselves as a bubble and all our lives we are growing and expanding, we can better understand when we hit those little bubbles that cause us to expand and take care of ourselves during times of expansion. If you don't grow, you lose a lot of your flexibility and adaptability. You also lose a bit of fun in life, but more about that later.

Boundaries and Our Need to Protect

I found that in being a Victim in my own life, I was not establishing clear and clean boundaries. Dr. Phil likes to say, "You teach people how to treat you." That used to make me angry hearing him say that because if people just followed the Golden Rule of treating others like they would like to be treated, it should be easy. I always assumed that because I lived by that rule, others would too. Not necessarily true. I remember one time I was on the verge of breaking up with a boyfriend. It seemed like I was doing all the giving and making excuses why he didn't seem capable of giving back or meeting my needs. He was good at excuses himself so I had to wonder why he needed my help with making more, but there I was, Miss Helpful. My excuses for him focused on the fact that he was busy in a high stress career and wasn't high energy like I was. I figured if I gave more, then he'd notice and feel bad and start to give back. I would have that reaction so he must too. We all want some sort of balance in giving and taking. I just thought I was being compassionate with people who couldn't give back as much in the moment. After all, it would happen down the line, right? As I ask my clients now, "Where is that written?" We all make the mistake of making assumptions that aren't true and never bother to look at them again to ask if those assumptions were valid. I got a big wakeup call the day that my boyfriend told me rather proudly that we were a good match. "You like to give and I like to receive," he announced. I nearly fell over. Here I was assuming one day my ship would come in and he would give me all the love and compassion I had been waiting for, whereas, he had found a Giver and he was content with being a Taker so in his mind he had a great companion. How on earth had I missed that? He has gone on in his life and married a woman, and this time he seems to work a bit harder at giving. It seems he found his assumption wasn't so on target either! I on the other hand watch carefully when I am doing all the giving. If it develops into a pattern, I'm gone or severely curtailing the time and energy that the relationship is taking. This pattern of one person giving more than another doesn't just happen in romantic relationships. It happens in relationships with your children too. You have a job to teach them to make sacrifices at times and to be giving. I know too many parents who have raised high maintenance princes and self-absorbed princesses. If they are that way, you didn't do your job as a parent.

So you have to teach your children how to create boundaries for when they come into contact with life's Takers and you have to have healthy boundaries yourself to model for your young adult. When I say *boundaries* I mean the lines we draw as to how we will allow ourselves to be treated and how we define respect. Parents in the past trampled over their children's boundaries like marauding invaders. They could be cruel with whippings and criticisms. They often were verbal and emotional bullies. The idea was compliance at any and all costs. As powerless beings, the message we got as children was that those in authority or in certain positions have the right to harm us. I dare say most of us are products of such mindsets. It had the added benefit to society of creating citizens who obeyed authority. Most of our society and other societies are based on this idea of having a place in the social hierarchy and obeying those in authority. However, too many young people, and the rest of us, have poor concepts of defining and protecting our personal boundaries out of deference to authority.

It all comes back to us parents needing to model good boundary definition and maintenance. If it looks like you have to heal yourself as you raise your children, you probably do need to do that. I did and still am doing it. I even have to tell my children when I've had a change in how I define myself or how I am constructing and protecting my boundaries. As with learning to take care of yourself, creating clear boundaries is part of that concept. You have to decide when you are not being respected or being heard. You will get a clear sign of an invasion of your boundary when you find yourself being angry with some comment or behavior just as Justin was with his boss. Your boundary line has been crossed. For some of us, that is the first awareness of where that boundary is. It is important when it happens to re-establish the boundary. If you think of a boundary as being similar to the property line between you and your neighbor, maybe a neighbor that you don't know or like very much, it is easy to be clearer on the concept. Sometimes your neighbor doesn't know they have crossed the boundary line either because they are busy or just pre-occupied. It may seem obvious to you but in some cases people really don't know where the boundary line is and need to be informed. For most of us, we have social mores that tell us general boundaries in dealing with others and then as we get to know each other, we can be more specific.

The hard part is that teens are just learning to create boundaries between each other and between family members. As parents we frequently invade the boundaries of our teens. They react the way we all would react if everyone was trampling over your property line, and that is with anger. Having grown up with parents who frequently violated my boundaries with harsh words and criticisms, I found that I had poorly defined boundaries for protecting myself. I wouldn't stop someone crossing the line until they were well within the backyard so to speak. At that point, people feel very threatened. The response is typical; you strike out hard to ward off the interloper. Explosive teens and young adults have frequently learned this from their parents. In our generation, you could never *talk back* which meant you couldn't defend yourself. We watched and saw that you struck back only when the invasion had gone too deep. If you ever watch the *Jerry Springer Show* with all of its drama and explosions and violence, this is the mode of dysfunction these people live in. They allow invasions that go too deep within the boundary line to become a frightening attack on who they are.

Chapter 8 Boundaries and Bubbles

I noticed with Justin early on that he had no defense but to lie or twist things if he thought he was being unfairly judged or was failing in some way. As happens frequently in alcoholic relationships or in highly dysfunctional relationships that have strong Victim, Persecutor, and Rescuer dynamics, the attacks between one another can be daily and horribly intense. Since his role had been primarily Victim, he had little recourse except to get very clever in verbally distracting his Persecutors. He was good at being evasive and making promises he would later avoid keeping just to get his family off his back. At one point early on when he was living with his aunt, she complained to me that he lied a lot. I had watched their interactions and noticed she never bothered to find out what he thought or wanted. She had an agenda for him to follow into successful adulthood and that was what she had done growing up. When he was living with me, I let him see that even if I didn't agree with his choices, I respected them and him. He no longer needed to be deceptive as a means of protecting himself. But he had to learn to figure out what his boundary lines were and to convey them clearly.

Often in families, we don't use polite niceties that we save for strangers. We trample over each other's yards and into each other's personal space like disrespectful robbers. My mother could be a gracious, compassionate, and humorous person. We as children got to see that at times while at other times she would be invading the very center of our hearts and souls with no awareness of the lovely places she was rampaging through. As an adult, I left and moved far away. I allowed her to interact with me on my terms and those involved being kind and respectful to me as she would be to a stranger. My one sister commented once that our mother was kinder to neighbors than she was to the rest of us. People would assume the same woman they knew was the one we experienced, also. If only my mother had known that the secret to strong, vital relationships with us would be to treat us with the same respect she treated our neighbors and set the expectations that we would do the same with her. With these insights and tools, she could have had the loving relationship she encountered with non-family members in her life. It saddens me when people say the <u>love</u> their children but they don't <u>like</u> them. What nonsense is that other than that boundaries have been disrespected and most likely both parties feel invaded and disrespected?

I used to listen to Justin talk to his mother in our kitchen on his phone while she was drinking. There would be much drama and insulting going on. Once Justin realized that now that he was no longer living under her roof he could *talk back*, and he let her receive the same insults that he had been given. This is back to the dysfunction model of Victim and Persecutor and leaves both parties feeling worn and upset. I explained to him that how I deal with alcoholic family members is not to talk to them when they are drinking. I had been told this by a recovering alcoholic and it saved me many upsetting phone calls that I used to tolerate. He had every right to make that choice and disconnect from his mother while she was drinking. I told him he simply needed to say that given she was drinking and being belligerent, he'd talk to her the next day when she wasn't drinking. I explained it could also work when things were going bad. Instead of fighting and getting into a dysfunctional Victim and Persecutor role, he could calmly say they needed to talk another time. Before long, this new boundary was being respected by his mother. At times she was too angry or drunk to adjust her behavior, but having the tool to react rationally in defending his boundary left him feeling much more in control and self-respecting. He also started to use this at work.

Anger outbursts are understandable when you are in junior high and haven't learned how to control your emotions yet, but in adulthood, they aren't acceptable. Yet many people continue to treat family members like this because it was how they grew up. If you remember, in the past, people were having children before age 25 when their brains were still growing. As older parents, we can bring a cooler head to the situation and need to as a way to model.

There are very simple tools that can be used to achieve this. First and foremost are the magic words, "please" and "thank you". As I said before, I use the words with all my young adults and other people. It provides a sense of good manners and dignity and brings that out in the person with whom you are interacting. I am always amazed at how people become much nicer given those simple little words of respect. Secondly, allow people to "save face". I always remember hearing about that concept in college. It seemed so strange to me but I was told by a girlfriend who was dating an Asian man that it was something that Americans had to learn to understand in dealing with Asian cultures. The concept really does speak to a basic human need. In saving face, if you find that someone is going to be put in an embarrassing situation by what they have said or done, you find a way to play it down or make it no big deal. Either you take the blame or find an excuse that makes them look better than is the actual situation.

When my sons were young, I let them blame me for not going to events they really didn't want to attend but were getting pressured to participate in. My oldest son, Adam, once had promised to attend his high school homecoming game with friends. Despite being a very social person, he didn't like to waste time at school sports that just didn't keep his interest or attend school dances where people were critical and gossiping about one another. He preferred just spending time with friends when he wasn't working or studying. One evening, Adam, his brother, and I were going to a local Mexican restaurant. I was very much looking forward to the dinner as I love Mexican food. We had just parked and gotten out of the car. Suddenly, Adam was ducking and weaving back to the car saying he didn't want to go there. I was taken aback wondering if he was sick or what was going on as he seemed so stressed. I was trying to find out why we were turning around so abruptly and I was very disappointed that maybe we wouldn't be able to eat there as I had my heart set on it. Finally, he blurted out that he had promised friends that he would go to the homecoming game and he saw some of those kids stopping nearby for coffee. Since he had no desire to go to homecoming and was thinking he'd find an excuse later for not showing, his excuse would be discredited by those who might see him going into the restaurant with his family. Yes, he probably could have handled peer pressure better than by agreeing to go to an event that he really hated attending. But the deed was done and hopefully he would learn his lesson on this. For the time being, I agreed to have us go elsewhere as long as I got to choose dinner out the next time. It is just so important in these formative social years to save face and I remembered that. If you can show that you are sensitive to these things, it puts extra credit in your parenting account. My sons know that I will take the blame to shield them from embarrassments. Isn't that what we all would want in our friends and loved ones? It was a small price to pay for me and a big deal for them.

If you can use the magic words and treat your teen with the kindness and respect that build healthy self-esteem and shows that you respect them, it will naturally come back to you. Whenever I am told that a teen is being rude and mean or abusive to their

Chapter 8 Boundaries and Bubbles

parents, I know that the chances are good that the behavior has been modeled by the parent. However, sometimes it isn't. Sometimes a "back message" is happening that explains the negative reaction. Often the person who is hearing an underlying message or a "back message" is reacting to that and we don't understand why when we aren't saying anything negative. I was listening recently to an interview with Deborah Tannen, author of a number of books on verbal communication. She has written the bestselling book, *You Just Don't Understand*, which dealt with the messages that men and women hear in their conversations with each other that go beyond the literal meaning of the words expressed. Now she has written another, *You're Wearing That? Understanding Mothers and Daughters in Conversation*. In the interview, she explained how our children hear implied criticism in our sometimes harmless statements. Other messages that they think they are hearing can also be seen by them as unrealistic expectations or demands. Past interactions have sensitized them to what they *think* you are saying.

Recently, my youngest son came home from school in a very angry mood. This isn't like Richard. He is generally a quiet and easy-going guy. I knew that he had become very political and seemed to have hit a point where he was explosive about the injustices of the world and suddenly I was treated to tirades I had never even imagined he considered. I remember myself being this volatile and idealistic as a teen. I was going to smash all the wrongs and the perpetrators and rescue their victims and change the world! As I am fond of telling my sons, if you think you have life figured out, then enjoy it. Life is going to kick you in the rear and wake you up and dispose of your fantasy sooner or later. But it is great that Richard had this passion and drive.

Richard's tirade about how ridiculous school was and how irrelevant his classes were (to which I agreed to some extent) seemed extreme and I thought he needed some things to consider and soften in his opinion. But then he started to attack me! I had been an honor student, third in my class of about 300 plus students at my high school. I had told Richard when he started middle school that I thought he was equally as gifted and competitive. He had labored for a while under this high standard and one time told me almost tearfully that it was too much stress and strain living up to my ideal. He had said to me then that I should trust that he was doing his best and that he emotionally beat himself up and was far more critical of his short-comings than I could ever be. I told him then that yes, I would trust that he is giving his best. But now he was doing it again, yelling and complaining that school is so much harder than it ever was for me, and teachers were more inaccessible and lazy and so on. I told him that was it. He had crossed the line in attacking me. I was calm about it. I refused to speak further until he apologized. I also pointed out that he didn't work eight hours a week and keep house for my mother and watch five younger siblings as I had done so the comparison was not equal even though I would give him the point that school work is much more difficult today. Once he apologized, I found out that he had failed a test in his advanced math class because he had made the wrong assumption and applied the wrong format to his analysis. Instead of partial credit for all the work he had done, he got no credit, an "F". This is where we needed to problem solve and that is exactly what I want you to do in emotional situations. Calm down, figure out the real problem, and solve it. Work the problem, not the person. Believe me, in situations where you feel attacked or your boundaries are invaded this is difficult. But it is doable.

For him it meant dropping the class, which was no easy task in his high school. But our motto is, "if there is a will there is a way." In problem solving, you need to use your head and push past usual solutions. There was a class at our local community college he could still get into that he had some background interest in and it would look good on his transcript to have taken a college course. I thought that the high school would agree but they sure didn't make it easy. Still we succeeded. He was relieved as the math class had been incredibly stressful for a long time. He apologized again and I refused his apology until I had a promise from him. He was never to be a Victim again on this issue of doing as well as me academically. We both lived under different times and I trusted that he would put forth his best effort. I had only set that expectation because when his older brother had started middle school, he assumed that a "C" average was all he needed to aspire to now that he was under a grading system. I had to set the expectation that a "C" is about the lowest I wanted to see, not the usual. So I thought I was just setting out reasonable expectations for Richard when he started the grading system, but in his mind he heard a harsh and critical parent. He needed to let go of that critical parent in his head. It wasn't me. Too many of us run critical tapes from long ago that no longer have validity. Help your young adults and teens leave those behind, as you should if you have any replaying from the past. He also had to bring problems to me to solve, not do all this smoke screen behavior about what wasn't the problem. We would work as a team and not get worn out. We would work the problem not the person. This again is the message you want to give—team work. That I could stand back and mentor him through high school pressure and be his coach was freeing for us both.

What was freeing for me was that I heard the back message in my head and didn't act on it. He was upset and worried that getting a bad grade in his class was going to compromise his getting into the college of his dreams. This wasn't about me. It was his fear. Remember that anger is fear, hurt, or frustration. His tirade was about a frightened young man watching his dreams slip away. I didn't allow my boundary to be compromised; I refused to go forward in that disrespectful tone he had with me. Just as I had taught Justin not to carry on conversations with his alcoholic mother in her drunken state, none of us need to move forward when our boundaries are being invaded. Showing respect for your boundaries will teach your young adults the same so that they aren't compromised by abusive bosses or significant others. This is a very important skill. It also creates a healthy dynamic and gets us away from the dysfunctional modes of Persecutor, Victim, and Rescuer.

Another very common area of boundary invasion that I see cropping up over and over is parental expectations of contact. While it seems common that many teens move into mono syllables in answering questions about their day and life, others do connect more frequently. I know one friend whose in-laws expected at least weekly check-ins from their adult children. Not very good at conversations, they didn't want anything too personal, just a check in as if they were children coming home after school. Also, there was some expectation that the younger generation had to pick up the phone and do the check-in. The parents were insulted if they had to call just to say *hi*. I have heard of this with others so perhaps it was some sort of older generation etiquette that came into being when the phone was a relatively new instrument. But I have encountered many parents in my generation who also have certain expectations of frequent contact. There are no rules about this despite what older generations seemed to think. Relationships are negotiated and forms of communication are individual. In

72

dealing with people, I ask the other person how they best like to be contacted. I know some prefer phone calls while others prefer e-mail. I am more of an e-mail person while my sons, Adam and Richard, are both more phone call types. Justin is more a phone type but has moved into texting, a sort of combination of phone and e-mail. It is important to work out some sort of agreement as to how often you both want the contact. To make up unilateral rules is not respecting the other person's needs and time. Teens and young adults are balancing a lot on their plates and they are in growth phases. They may not provide the sort of contact you prefer but it is a place to start and hopefully it will evolve into something more frequent. Required daily phone calls are needy and often suffocating, but it comes up quite a bit more than I thought. Usually, this is the demand of the parent. As I told several young adult clients, that is parental anxiety that you only feed if you allow it to go on. Even parents can be neurotic and need boundaries set for their behavior.

These early years of adulthood are characterized generally by pulling away to manage life. I have had to counsel several moms and it tends to be more moms that think infrequent contact means that they are forgotten. One mother was very irritated that her daughter, with whom she had been so close and so heavily involved in her life, now didn't return daily phone calls fast enough, and the young woman preferred to be with friends rather than spend time with mom anymore. This is very natural. This is so hard not to take personally but it isn't personal. It is a phase. This is also a time to ask what sort of relationship you have had with them. Were you the Drill Sergeant parent, authoritarian, making decisions in their lives, giving orders based on your experiences? Were you the Helicopter parent as the mother was who wanted daily contact? Are they putting a bit of silence and distance between you so they can be themselves and live their own choices? Even with the kids who have returned home, I hear how they *disappear* off with friends or sleep a lot. Both are ways to avoid you and find their own path. They need to pull away and your job now is to find out how to fill your life differently now that it isn't your job to run their lives.

It is also possible that you have nagged or criticized for way too long. Work the problem, not the person. You will only drive them away when you do that sort of behavior. Nagging has to stop. It is demoralizing. Remember what Dr. Phil said about it taking ten *atta boys* to make up for one hurtful criticism? Look at where you have been as a parent during these teen years and make a fresh start to be calm and become that Counselor parent, that coach that is on their team. Understand that communication in these years may be limited but it is easy when they know you respect them and their boundaries.

Bubbles and Goose Bumps

Now that we understand the need for healthy boundaries and protecting them and thus our core selves, let's discuss growth. In one Tony Robbins seminar that I attended, Tony said if you aren't growing, you are dying. We have an instinctive need to expand ourselves and our skills. It makes us adaptable to situations and changing periods in our lives. I like the analogy of bubbles that I believe I learned at Tony Robbins' "Unleash the Power Within" seminar. Tony said that you can think of our personalities like balloons that expand over life. That makes a lot of sense in that some of us like to expand a lot and some of us like to expand a little. In my town, there is a young teen, Mark, who goes with his mom to restaurants that allow him to perform and he makes balloon animals and items. You've all seen these balloon artists who twist and turn long and short and round balloons into things in a matter of seconds. Mark is really good at this and makes a fair bit of change for his balloon objects. One of the things you note is when Mark blows up one part, he can control a small bit of air to make another part of the balloon puff into a new part. We are sort of like those balloons in our personality growth. I like the idea of some sections expanding depending on the control of air. The air goes into the area of least resistance and the balloon stretches and that section fills out and a new section expands. The same happens with an air mattress being blown up. A section fills and then it rounds out the area more. We are balloons with all these goose bump expansions that need to fill out with more air. These are the skills and experiences we need to grow and became more of who we are.

However, when you hit a big goose bump expansion, there is a natural fear of the balloon bursting. Is that area too thin to accommodate so much air? Will there be expansion to new areas of least resistance to give the balloon animal the shape it needs? A new job, a new marriage, a new house, a move, a new baby, all of these are big goose bumps or, better said, they are big expanders on the balloon surface of who we are. In my Power Point presentation for talks, I have a picture of a round circle with this large poked up part of the circle that looks like it could burst the circle. Smaller changes are mere goose bumps on the surface but this is a dramatic expansion. We all decide when a change looks like a goose bump on the circle of who we are but there are some things that are so large and expansive they overwhelm us. We can't even imagine how we will look once the area fills in smoothly and the entire balloon is larger in size. For us our old identity, our old shaped personality is threatened with becoming something we can't imagine. Most people will tell you that once you go through some of these expanders, you aren't the same. You have new skills and new ways of looking at things once you have gone through the growth. Areas that weren't initially involved have grown too. For young adults and teens this is a frightening and an overwhelming experience. It is important to help them negotiate through these life skills that most of us no longer find intimidating. As soon as I get resistance in my coaching, I know that there may be fears of too much expansion and there is a threat of bursting that is slowing things down. At least that is how I work with it. I'm big on hand holding people through changes and to get them to see the expander as a goose bump they can handle. With an outsider along, people can find ways to make the transition they desire by working past the fear and overwhelm. This extra support means all the difference.

When parents want their teens and young adults to get jobs, I'm always shocked at how little support they give to making that happen. It takes us back to the idea that they look like adults, therefore they must be adults and can run their lives like adults. It isn't true. Remember their brains are still functioning more like a child's than like an adults. Discuss jobs ideas with your young adult and then take them to fill out applications or obtain applications or sit down and fill out applications. When Justin got his last job as a visual merchandiser, he did it on his own. However, in his initial months with me, I literally took him out to a number of places to inquire about jobs and apply. I have done that with my own two sons, Adam and Richard. They get the feel for it. In doing this skill set acquisition, if you want your young adult to do it, get busy going with them. You are the leader, you are their coach. Get in the game with

Chapter 8 Boundaries and Bubbles

them. This is also great for building bonds. Whether I'm teaching driving or job-hunting, the funny stories and memories that come out of these moments connect me with others like nothing else. If you can bring humor, calmness, patience, and a sense of compassionate support to the experience, it will enrich everyone. It isn't just your children growing, it is you too. You are becoming a better leader and a better coach. Don't forget, you are the role model for them. How you handle these instances guides how they will approach and handle them.

If you are hitting resistance, if you perceive fear that it is too much to ask, break down the task to smaller tasks. Little goose bumps rather than bubble breaking larger ones, lessen the fear factor. Remember Cindy, the 20-year-old woman learning to drive? Even though she had gotten her learner's permit as a teen, the thought of getting her license some four years later sent her into a panic. Three times she found excuses to back out of going for her written test to get the permit. In her mind, the permit was the beginning of stress and failure. I had to get her to only look at the permit. Help your young adult or teen to learn to focus on the little step not the entire project under hand. One day at a time, one step at a time. This is the other thing to note. If you are repeating a step over and over, don't yell; understand that more is going on. I didn't get mad; I just knew that I would have to gently and firmly persist. One trick for teaching them how to only look at the step in front of them is to give them an out. For example, with Cindy, you might explain that she is only getting her permit and she doesn't have to get her license, she could just practice for a few years, but at least she would have the permit. By saying these sorts of things, the big plan recedes into time and fades into the background. All you are looking at, the only real goal is to get the permit. Of course, once you have the permit, aren't you going to naturally want to get to the license? But don't go that far out in planning at least in talking about it or worrying about it. Just the immediate step is all you want. I didn't find out this was the way for me to handle overwhelm in my own life until the last seven years. Just do one thing at a time, and don't go down the road of horrible outcomes and failures. Feel good about one thing accomplished. One foot in front of the other and one day at a time is where you want to focus. Be patient, break down the process into small steps, and don't connect them to the big overwhelming picture. Leave them completed in and of themselves, one small step for now and that's good enough. The same goes for getting jobs. When my son, Adam, went to work at a local drug store chain, he always knew if it didn't work out time-wise or otherwise, he could quit. Show up to your challenge, try it on for a while, and leave it if it isn't working. Come back to it another day or move to something else. This is how to deal with big challenges and overwhelm in life.

Now the other piece to this is, once your young adult is doing all of this and moving through the challenge, you need to give them down time and space to grow into their new bubble size. As we expand our identities, it takes energy and we need some time to recover from the growth and live with the *new* us. I would find myself getting so excited at all the growth I was seeing in Justin, I would want to push out to the next challenge immediately. As I would tell Cindy in her driving experiences, some days I pushed too much in all the skills I was going for in the day and she would become worn out and not perform as well with the last few challenges. That was my fault. We needed time for her brain to accommodate the new synapse connections. It is important that you back off a bit and encourage your teens and give them credit for all they are accomplishing. From their perspective, the tasks to completing the skill loom

75

much more before them than the completed challenge. Growing is energy consuming. Recognize that and praise what has happened. Give them some breathing space along the way.

And that's it on bubbles. There are only two rules. Help your young adult break down and accomplish small goose bumps with each new skill, and secondly, give them credit and space to reflect upon the new the new person they become. It is a matter of pacing but demanding more creates more setbacks. Gently moving forward a goose bump at a time is the way to go. ⌾

Chapter 9 Tools For Knowing Your Young Adult

When our children are little, we are so enraptured with getting to know them. We want to know what irritates them, what their favorite foods, TV shows, games, and toys are, all of it. But by the time they are teens, we pretty much know them by their accomplishments, i.e. their academic standing, participation in extra-curricular sports, outings with friends. But who are they as people?

Since my degree is in psychology, I have a lot of friends in psychology. There are lots of ways to characterize personalities. There are amateur ways to do it such as by horoscopes and astrological signs. Patterns exist just as we talked about in personality types in dysfunctional relationships. Those personalities in transactional analysis were Victim, Persecutor, and Rescuer. Recently, I took the Myers-Briggs personality test to find out what my personality type is in that format. My dear friend from college, Dr. Deborah Orlowski, has always found it helpful in understanding people. In that system there are 16 personality types. My brother swears by the nine personality types in the Enneagram, which has its origins in spiritual systems. I follow the tools used by Tony Robbins since I've attended all the seminars in his Masters University and his Leadership Academy. What I like is the simplistic approach that we all can grasp quickly and use effectively. Tony uses Neuro-Linguistic Programming (NLP) and Human Needs Psychology, which he developed. Here is a quick overview of the two systems.

Visuals, Auditories, and Kinesthetics

We've already spoken of the three roles of dysfunction in transactional analysis, the Victim, the Perpetrator, and Rescuer. They are easy to spot since so many of us come from long lines of family dysfunction. These always made a great deal of sense to me. However, another ah-ha moment I had in attending one of Tony Robbins' seminars was his discussion of Neuro-Linguistic Programming (NLP) founded in the 1970's by John Grinder and Richard Bander. In NLP, how people perceive the world is influenced by his or her choice of focus and the things a person tell themselves about their world and reality. If you tell yourself that you will never be rich, guess what? You will never be rich! I have a single female friend who says, "There are no good men available" and that really is her reality. When students start looking to go off to college, I frequently hear them say the things that they learned from their parents, such as they could never go to this school or that school. It is also perpetrated by high school counselors and by their peers. Even my son, Adam, thought the same thing. He never thought he could get into the academically more challenging University of California schools, so he never applied. Now, two years after going to a California State University, he is transferring and realizing he can get in if he plans it right. It is as much about picking the right major as having a certain grade point average. Yet colleges pick from a broad spectrum of grades and personalities. It doesn't hurt to give it a shot.

I read just last year that the people who devise one of the more widely used college entrance exams, the SAT, had some errors in grading their new formats. People who had done well scored lower than they should have, and people who didn't do so well scored higher than they should have. One disappointed, highly academic student in a *People Magazine* article bemoaned the fact that they had wanted to get into a prestigious college and never tried because he thought his score wasn't in the higher stratosphere that he assumed was required. This student should have tried. He defeated himself before anyone else could. My children and I call this "Poor Dad" thinking from the book *Rich Dad, Poor Dad* by Robert Kiyosaki. Both Tony Robbins and Robert Kiyosaki say the key to success is to ask yourself the questions of *how* to get what you want before saying it can't happen and not trying. I have found the most amazing things start to happen just by asking the question "how can I make this happen" and then being open to the ideas that start to come. When you start walking toward your dreams, paths and people show up that you had no idea were ever there.

By knowing yourself and your young adult or teen you can maximize these results and these approaches to success as you define it. NLP talks about how we focus. We all have approaches in how we process the world and NLP bases the patterns of approach on the five physical senses. The majority of the population falls into Visual, Auditory, or Kinesthetic groupings, although there are very small and rarer groups based on smell and taste. With each of these groups a personality type also emerges. As I sat in the Tony Robbins seminar on introductory NLP, Tony brought people up onto the stage to demonstrate how the interactions between the different types are colored by their processing preference. It was quite interesting to watch how the energy levels and personalities of the groupings differed and yet seemed very much alike within each group.

I, like Tony, am a Visual processor. I need to see things. I need to visualize things. Visuals tend to be much more animated, high-energy sorts of people. About 60 percent of people are Visuals. What I found amazing was that my sons, Adam and Richard, aren't Visuals. Adam is an Auditory and Richard is a Kinesthetic. I was so stunned. I had assumed they were like me! Auditories process the world by hearing. I knew Adam was an Auditory because he had an unbelievably high cell phone bill. This guy was always talking. It was his biggest complaint from teachers since he was in kindergarten, that he talked too much. He was always being *too social*. About 20 percent of the population is Auditory. They are high-energy people too, but a little less so than visuals. The Kinesthetic is someone guided by feeling. They tend to be slower, quieter people who love being alone. My youngest son, Richard, is a Kinesthetic. In observing the three of us, I have concluded that Kinesthetics have what I call poorer filters of input than Visuals or Auditories. It is easy to overwhelm them with too much. They seem to have a heightened sensitivity to the world around them and need more quiet time to just be. Visuals seem to seek out more stimuli. Perhaps we have thicker filters to what is going on around us and need more input to stay stimulated. The Auditory likewise seem to seek out more stimuli in an auditory way hence Adam's high phone bill. These are just my perceptions over the last few years living with all three types in my house.

Chapter 9 Tools For Knowing Your Young Adult

At this point, you may be wondering what the heck all this is about. In interacting with others, it is important to communicate effectively. We are trying to reach our children in all of this and hopefully have them reach us. I have found NLP extremely useful in all of my interactions. When I came home after my seminar, I sat my sons down and explained to them what I had learned. It was crystal clear from how we three chose movies to go to that the different modalities were in play. I would always love the theatres with the big screens. The huge IMAX screens that are three stories tall are about right for me. If only I had them in my home! However, Adam preferred the better sound system. I didn't even know there was a difference in movie theatres until he explained the quality of sound to me in our different theatres. Richard didn't care. He was there for the camaraderie. Now that I knew these differences I could see how my parenting wasn't the best for Richard as a child. I felt really bad about how I over scheduled Richard as a child when he truly needed more down time. When I put him in summer camp, he seemed stressed and at one time was so tearful about going. Like most parents, I assumed that my kids processed the world as I did. It had lead Richard several times as a child to break out in tears from all the stress and left me baffled as Adam seemed to do well with the same sort of schedule. I told Richard that we would do better in understanding his need for down time and his preferred slower pace for things. However, he needed to understand our drive and high energy because the world is built by Visuals and Auditories who expect others to be just like them. It really helped us to understand one another and communicate more effectively.

NLP has helped us enormously with figuring out how to interact. When we went to Europe for Adam's graduation from high school, I had several family friends throughout Europe to stay with and, given that my sons were getting ready to go off to college over the next few years, I thought I would give them a taste of a number of different countries. Down the road we could return to favorites and spend more time. This was a buffet of countries trip. So we spent a few days in the Netherlands with Maria and her family, a few days in Switzerland with Anne and her family, several days on the French Riviera and a few days in Paris with Anne, then off to England for a few days with Victoria and her son. We did it all in less than two weeks. For a Visual, this is easy, even fun. An Auditory might enjoy it also, but a Kinesthetic will be burned out! I tried to factor in down time, a movie, a quiet tour somewhere, and things of that nature, but in no way was Richard left alone to have the down time he really needed. He was ever the good sport about it though. Then he started to have visual changes in that his vision seemed foggy at times. I told him he was doing really well given the high stress to a Kinesthetic and reassured him his vision would be normal when he got some rest back home. He asked me if he could see the eye doctor to make sure and I reassured him that I would schedule an appointment. We didn't need it as he was fine after a few quiet days at home. Other parents might have yelled at Richard for not being more enthusiastic or causing hassles. But we all understood Richard and tried to accommodate him and he tried to keep up and have a good attitude even though he was more stressed. If you criticize your young adult or teen for who they are, it is damaging. They can't change; they can accommodate, but that is an effort and it needs to be recognized. He was very giving to us and we appreciated it.

The irony is that many Kinesthetics marry Visuals, according the one instructor I took a class from in the subject matter. I found that pretty funny as I was married to two Kinesthetic men in my past marriages. I am a high level sort of Visual, which is one reason I don't think it worked out well for me. However, I have observed that we can cross over into the other categories sometimes if needed. You can have a tendency toward one modality but work fine in another. Adam can work well as a Visual. His natural tendency is Auditory but he can function very well at the Visual level. Richard can function very well at the Auditory level even though his tendency is Kinesthetic. I have had to work hard to understand Kinesthetics. It is so different from me. However, you can learn to function well with a different modality because I find that more Kinesthetics are drawn to me. NLP has taught me a lot.

These differences show up in a number of ways you might not think of at first. Having two young, college-aged men, it came up when deciding on types of colleges to attend. When picking colleges, I like large college campuses as does my son, Adam. We need the stimulus of lots going on and lots of people. Adam's father, Harold, is a Kinesthetic. He can function well as a Visual but poorly as a Auditory. Harold's mother is also a Kinesthetic and used to complain that she was always trying to get Harold out of his room. She seemed to have wanted Harold to be an Auditory like his father or his brother. It makes Kinesthetics feel less than normal to be pushed in this manner. Discounting the personality of a Kinesthestic like that is much like how schools used to make left handed children write with their right hands. We would never to think to do that now, but the perception then was that there was something wrong with left handed people and they had to be corrected. Even with Richard as a child, I thought maybe he had a tendency to be lazy like his father. Neither are lazy but they are more productive in quiet moments and don't need to be so high energy. Once we appreciate the personality, we maximize everyone's enjoyment of themselves and ourselves. Not surprisingly, Harold encouraged our oldest son, Adam, toward smaller, tighter knit, quieter colleges which would have been his preference. He found himself as a young man going to very large colleges and overwhelmed in many respects. Having that in mind when I took Richard to look at colleges, I noticed he liked intermediate sized colleges or colleges surrounded with land and rural aspects. It is the calm a Kinesthetic seems to love.

Just as with shopping for colleges for our teens and young adults, the focus in finding a good job for your young adult is based on their inclinations. We never think of these things but it is a way to figure out the optimum match. My oldest son, Adam, is Auditory and he does very well with sales. One summer, he worked for a local drug store chain. He didn't like it. He discovered that passive sales like that didn't engage his personality and make it rewarding. He likes a more active sales job of getting out there and making sales and working closely with others to develop sales strategies. So we focused on what elements he liked in that job and what he didn't. You can only know that by doing the job. However, his brother Richard quickly learned he liked the quieter jobs. Richard's father is a doctor, a radiologist who has a lot of quiet time reading x-rays. It's a good fit except for the constant interruptions. The Kinesthetic personality seems to work best away from the hustle and bustle. Finding the right job area has to be more than picking a college major. You need to be able to match it to your personality. Keep this in mind when you figure out who your young adult is and what the better jobs are for them. Exploration of types of jobs in the early teen years is critical. If there is one factor for why we have so many young people at home it is that we took away the thousands of years of teens working and replaced it with this passive existence of study. It is too way too late to start that upon graduation from college but more on that later.

Humans Needs Psychology

Once I have figured out the primary processing and communication modality someone is, I can move into a bit more complicated area. In NLP we had three primary processing styles, six if you also try to figure out what the secondary category is for that person. For example, I am primarily a Visual but secondarily a high functioning Auditory. Now to add to the mix is Tony Robbins' Human Needs psychology factors. Again this is a way to get to know someone and it is a way to understand how best to coach your young adult.

Tony says that we all have six human emotional needs, but we tend to be driven the most by two or three of those. The six human needs are 1) security, 2) variety, 3) love and connection, 4) significance (I call it *ego*), 5) growth, and 6) contribution. When you figure out what two or three primary needs are most important to you, it will tell you a lot about the choices you make. Tony also says that sometimes the needs are in conflict and that can cause problems. For example, if you have *security* as one of your primary drives, you are less likely to have variety as a top three drive. But it can happen and then you have an internal conflict of trying to have security while still looking for variety. Love and connection focuses on others external to you, which will conflict a bit with significance, where the focus is self centered. I don't mean that ego is necessarily bad as we tend to think when we say, "He has a big ego." It is also a good thing to have an ego that is self confident and healthy. As with all else in life, it is about balance. Likewise, contribution is what you are giving to the world, to others, while growth focuses inward on expanding your bubble.

One thing that Tony notes is that when you meet three needs at a high level, you get an addiction. It makes sense that, since we require all six of these needs, meeting such a high number with someone or something will feel great to us. It can also not be such a good thing. For example, overeating meets the needs of security for one. After all, isn't that what is meant by "comfort food?" Secondly, it meets the need for variety as there are so many choices we have in our country to have fresh everything year round as well as fast food or readymade food. It can foster love and connection as we use food as a time to socialize and be together, so right there three of the needs are met. Is it any wonder that we have an obesity problem in this country? When you know what drives people in these areas, you can also motivate them and talk about the things that matter most to them. Growth is a big drive for me so I am always seeking out new ways to expand who I am through different experiences. I also am driven by variety. With those two I am willing to take risks that other people aren't. I'm also a good person to do new things with because I offer security and variety to others. I know variety is big with my son, Adam, and growth is big with Richard. Knowing these things, I can better help them see how their needs are being met or not being met with various choices.

I have to say that I have also noticed that for almost every Kinesthetic I have known, security is one of their primary driving forces. But that is mere observation on my part. Richard also likes variety so it gets him out of his room so to speak. In general though, Kinesthetics like to stay in the same house, in the same job, and they like their routine. Knowing that, I sent Richard almost every summer somewhere on a trip during his high school years. I wasn't trying to be mean; I just felt that, once out on his own, his inclination to travel would most likely not be a priority. This was my chance to expand his horizons. I have heard parents say that they don't force their kids to take advantage of these opportunities, but remember, their brains are still growing and they can't adequately make good judgments about these things. I myself was an exchange student when I was 16 for a summer in Switzerland. I initially didn't want to go either. I thought it would be better to do as I always did and earn money for my fall school wardrobe. My mother was furious with me trying to pass up the opportunity and ordered me to go. It was a profound experience and she was absolutely right. Travel to other countries gives you perspective you can't get any other way. So I felt that, given his personality, Richard may not be inclined to travel as an adult and this was my opportunity to expand his vistas now. I didn't order him as my mother had done me, but rather pointed out how it would look good on college transcripts and make up for deficiencies in extra-curricular activities or grade point average. It usually didn't take much more than that and some advance planning to make him feel more secure. Now he is very interested in travel. It feeds his need for variety and he has made new friends on all of his travel adventures so that he satisfies the need for love and connection.

We were in Europe when he was 15 because of his brother's high school graduation, but the following year Richard went with a group to Israel, and the year after that to Peru with his Spanish teacher and about ten classmates. While I had him under my wing, I knew it would expand his personality bubble and it has. I knew it would be hard being a Kinesthetic in both the tour groups as those things start very early and are very busy cramming in tourist sites and visits. That leaves very little down time and early days. Richard also had significant phase delay in his sleep patterns so that he would not usually getting to bed until 2:00 or 3:00 a.m. But he has a good attitude about things and did well. Although in Israel he suffered from a bit of dehydration early on and in Peru he acquired a bad case of Montezuma's revenge, he persevered. He came away from these trips loving to see new places and people. He had learned how different cultures operate and how our culture is viewed outside of our own country.

My father was a Kinesthetic and he stayed in the same job for over 30 years. This is what you will find with Kinesthetics. Security means a great deal to them. In most of the Visuals and Auditories that I know, variety is high on the list somewhere. Variety is huge for me. I see it as freedom. Security can start to bore me and suffocate me. This is what Tony Robbins says of the conflict of the two. With security you start to get bored, it is predictable. With variety, you start to feel unstable and nothing feels safe and secure enough. Can you imagine now a father for whom security was a primary drive with a daughter for whom variety is a driving force? That was my father and me. If you don't understand these things, you may misunderstand your young adult or teen. I was a great mom for my oldest son, the Auditory, in that like me he has variety as one of his primary drives so we went to parks and museums, all sorts of places when he was little. However, I was terrible for my younger son, who I was constantly signing up for a multitude of activities. In my perception, he should like them since I did. When he kept complaining and getting very upset, I wondered if he had separation anxiety or something. It was only after I learned about the six human needs that I got it. If we take a trip together, I try to build in nature excursions and quiet time to make it enjoyable for him. A little variety goes a long way for him and he has learned to appreciate it.

Chapter 9 Tools For Knowing Your Young Adult

One of my best friends, Sean, picked me up from the airport after I attended the Tony Robbins seminar where I learned about this. I was so excited about figuring out my family and friends so that I could be a better person for them. When I listed them, Sean immediately said, "Security is the most important one, right?" I laughed and said, "I guess it is for you!" I would have never thought that at the time. Like me, he seemed to enjoy variety as one of his driving needs. He is also a Visual but a high functioning Kinesthetic. As my son, Adam, pointed out, the two driving needs for Sean have put him into conflict in many of his life's choices. I found that to be an interesting observation and one that is very true. We can have these conflicts. It is also important when you think you know what someone else's driving needs, to check it out with him or her. I have been very driven in my goals in life and that can look like a need for security. But for me, it is also a drive to get where I can have variety in my choices that involve security.

For example, I have a friend who is Kinesthetic and a high functioning Auditory in my perception. She has raised a family and is going into psychology to be a therapist. I too went into psychology to be a therapist. But our drives are very different. For me, it was growth, which is perhaps my greatest drive on a day-to-day basis. Psychology is great for growth because you learn so much dealing from with others. But also for me it satisfies the contribution drive as coaching or counseling advances another person's well being. For my friend, her motivation was significance, or, as I say, ego. She is the type of person who has to be the center of attention, who has to compete for attention in almost every social setting whether it is a party or a sales transaction. Being a therapist satisfies significance for her but it also satisfies her need for contribution. You see that in teachers, also. The best teachers are doing the job for contribution to our young and their future. Yet there are many who are in the job for their own self-focus of significance/ego. The ego driven teachers aren't necessarily doing it in a well-balanced way of ego as much as looking for attention for themselves and their egos. CEO's tend to be driven by significance/ego but the best CEO's are like Bill Gates. The philanthropic type of CEO brings their considerable talents to make a contribution to our world as well as to succeed in obtaining significance. There has been a tradition with many of our early philanthropists giving back to various causes. Richard read the biography of Andrew Carnegie and was impressed with the idea of the philanthropic creed of some of the early entrepreneurs who made fortunes in this country. We understand the person and their choices much better when we look at how they structure their priority of the six human needs. It helps to know the drives in you and in your young adults or teens. Like the processing modalities, if you are operating on the assumption that everyone is or should be like you, then your chances for success aren't great. When you try to impose your choices on others it is offensive and hurtful. This is especially so if that person is your own child.

My three primary drives are growth, contribution, and variety. I am very much a people person so everyone assumes that "love and connection" are in the top three for me. However, in the people for whom I have seen love and connection as a primary drive, it appears as almost a co-dependency to me. I'm sure it isn't but it looks different to me than how I relate. Keep in mind that we all fulfill these six human needs in differing amounts like in a food recipe. Add more flour to eggs and you get a cake. Add less flour and it starts to seem more like a crepe, not as substantial. We're all food recipes in that regard. The ingredients are there in differing amounts.

In all of these you can go from healthy avenues to unhealthy avenues. Perhaps because I have seen co-dependency, the unhealthy form of love and connection, it tends to make me gun shy. But in its healthy form, which I realized I practice daily, it is supportive and caring and makes life wonderful. Variety can become unhealthy by causing someone to be unreliable. Security can be very unhealthy, a stubbornness not to change even when it is called for and the slide to disaster continues despite all rationale thought to the contrary. Ego of course is very damaging to others if taken to the extreme. It is all consuming and insensitive to others. You may wonder about growth being at an unhealthy level, but this too can descend into a person becoming unreliable or self absorbed. Quite a few of us live in the extreme of contribution and I've been there. In its extreme, it is becoming an enabler or doormat. I am a recovering enabler and door mat. This one is very hard to break people of as they believe that any contribution and self-sacrifice is noble and good. It isn't and is unhealthy for the giver. As with all else in life, we need balance.

One of the most valuable things I got from my Tony Robbins' life coach is how to provide for another person's needs. Once you have figured out what their apparent top two or three needs are, you can work with them and have the best interactions by meeting those needs. In so many things, we tend to think the other person is just like us and we give them what we would want to be given. In Tony Robbins' seminar, "Date With Destiny", Tony recounts how he had a business partner at one point that he just didn't seem to be relating to well. Finally, one day it dawned on him that in the NLP system, he was a Visual and she was an Auditory. He made a point to call her more often and say things like, "I hear what you are saying" or "I hear where you are coming from." For a Visual you might say, "I see what you mean" or "I see your point." Likewise, for a Kinesthetic, you might say, "I feel that." Tony recounted that the partner said she felt like they were really communicating and understanding one another like they never had before. She felt heard. For myself, I have a lot of difficulty with people driven by significance or ego. My father and three of my siblings have that as a huge part of who they are. Needless to say, they live in the extreme part of ego where it is dysfunctional. They are the "right fighters" as Dr. Phil calls them. They need tons of attention and there is nothing more invigorating to these people than winning a fight, being right, and making the other person feel little or stupid. It means they are superior. Unfortunately, they tend to create the transactional triangle of Victim, Persecutor, and Rescuer and as Persecutors they are very ego driven. To the degree that you can get them to stop the dysfunctional roles by feeding their ego in a healthy way and by giving them compliments when they make good points, they can be more healthy in their ego needs. We all want to succeed, even the "right fighters". The trick when you have a young adult or teen driven by significance/ego, is to give them more responsibility and praise for accomplishments. They need to be making more decisions and being responsible for the outcome at this age anyway. If they make a mistake, find a positive way to frame the outcome. If they can be right while recognizing that things didn't go according to plan, then they will be less defensive which is where "right fighting" is born.

I never thought I could keep all of these categories straight, let alone use them while helping someone to problem solve. But the more you use it in everyday life to maximize your contacts and interchanges, the more helpful it will be in defusing situations. If you have a young adult at home, you need to defuse things and get a

Chapter 9 Tools For Knowing Your Young Adult

plan that they can get behind. These personality systems are ways to understand another. I know some have not born up under scientific scrutiny but it seems if you use something to start the dialogue and show interest in knowing the other person, that is more than half of the solution. You need to work the problem and get the ball moving forward. Don't get married to an end result. Plans need to be changed frequently as you discover how they work for the personality. That is a good thing. Stay flexible and observe the personality of yourself and your teen or young adult.

For example, my son Richard, the Kinesthetic, was asked about taking acting lessons. We got the sales call from John Robert Powers and I thought it might help him be more outgoing. Remember, this was when I didn't realize that he was a Kinesthetic and I, Ms. Totally Outgoing, thought anything less was a problem. As he took classes and developed a sense of confidence and interaction, *poise* as they called it in the old days, we began to wonder about his trying out for commercials or sit-coms or the like. Then one day he commented to me that he didn't want to pursue anything that could lead to possible fame. My adopted son, Justin, had thought fame was the end all and be all and I didn't see it as a problem. Then we discussed what Richard perceived about fame that he didn't like and that was the loss of privacy and the constant judgment of one's work and personality. If you are driven by significance/ego then it seems ideal to be famous, but if you are a quiet Kinesthetic, fame looks like a high price to pay for lack of down time and privacy. If security is important to you, then how do you handle all the stalkers and the paparazzi that follow you making your life very insecure? What happens to a sense of security at that point? These are things to learn and reflect on in relation to your personality. I am glad Richard tried and found out just how much he wanted to do or not do in media and acting life because the lessons he learned have left him a polished speaker and a poised young man, even if it didn't net him a career. It did a lot for him that we hadn't planned on. Sometimes we need to appreciate the lesson in something even if it isn't turning out the way we wanted.

The great thing about all of these personality attributes is that it gives you a starting place for conversation. One thing I have heard parents complain about over and over is how little their teens and young adults converse with them. The parents ask, "How are things?" and the response is "fine," even if they are in total crisis. What is happening in those situations is that there has been a long history of the parent either not hearing or listening to their teen or young adult or, if they have listened, they are quick to judge, criticize, or advise. In short, for them, there is a back message to anything you say that is more about how they aren't measuring up to what you want. It isn't too late to learn to converse. Use these or any other favorite personality systems to sit down and figure out who you are and who they are. I was pleasantly surprised to find out how enthusiastic my son Adam was about variety being his driving need. It explained a lot and let me know that when it comes to change, he will be easy to inspire. Justin likewise is big on variety, but because of his childhood, his need for security was frequently threatened. It has to be a fine balance when inspiring him. He needs to feel secure in obtaining his need for variety.

As you see, by learning about your young adult's personality, you can better sell ideas or inspire new paths and directions. This is what you want to do. Inspire not demand. Sell rather than dictate. This approach validates the other person no matter if they are a friend, a co-worker, your teen or adult child. We almost all are the walking wounded of our childhoods. It is rare to find it otherwise. If you can inspire and sell your ideas, then you will find a dialogue beginning. My Kinesthetic son knows that he is respected for who he is. Even though his father was raised by a Kinesthetic mother, she didn't see that in her son and kept trying to change him. When people try to change you, it implies you aren't good enough being who you are. In the former Good Parents Inc.'s booklet, "Three Steps To Parenting Teens", Joe Connolly, an award winning parent educator, did an excellent job explaining how to listen, how to turn conflict into opportunity, and how to listen with love and understanding. This has to be the shift if you are to motivate your young adult or teen to independence. The tools are there, you have to shift your expectations and experiences.

I strongly urge you to sit down and have an easy discussion about these three NLP processing modalities (the Visual, Auditory, and Kinesthetic) and the six human needs priorities. Make it an exchange of what you think they are and see what they think you are. It will be enlightening and a way to create new appreciation and new strategies. But let's add one more minor way to categorize needs and personalities which is helpful to your relationship as a whole. That is the languages of love.

Finding a Language of Loving Support

When I was divorced, I read a ton of relationship books. One that really impressed me was written by a man who seemed to understand the emotional aspects of relationships. The book is *The Five Languages of Love*, by Gary Chapman. Although the focus of that book is the language of love that speaks to you from your mate and finding their language, he has since written others, including one for children and one for teens. It makes sense that if we feel loved, we often feel supported. When you feel emotionally supported, it is easy to attempt new life challenges and drive through the hard ones. We are emotional animals no matter how much we all would be like my favorite Star Trek characters, Mr. Spock and Data.

In the book, Mr. Chapman lays out the five languages of love, which are 1) words of affirmation, 2) quality time, 3) receiving gifts, 4) acts of service, and 5) physical affection. When we know what our language is, we look to receive it from our loved ones and the other languages don't seem to matter. When parents say that they don't feel *appreciated*, often what they are saying is their language of love isn't present. As with most things, we all tend to think that what our language is must be what the other person's language will be. Again, we give what we want to receive.

This is another good place for dialogue building with your teen or young adult. I realized after reading Mr. Chapman's book that almost none of the languages of love were present in my failed marriages. What a surprise! I also realized that almost none were present in my relationship with my parents. It got me to start thinking, about my languages and the languages of my friends and family. For me, the top one is acts of service, having someone do things to help me out. Second is physical affection, a hug, a pat, a hand on the shoulder; the connection to another feels warm. Justin and I have spoken of this in figuring out what would be our ideal partners. It was no surprise to me that quality time is his top one. I have learned that he likes to do things together frequently and, being an Auditory, he calls almost every day, sometimes two or three times a day, which is also a version of quality time. Before I understood these

Chapter 9 Tools For Knowing Your Young Adult

personality traits, I might have been irritated, now I can relax and take them for what they are—his emotional conduits for being loved and supported.

My *daughter*, Gina is physically affectionate. That is her top love language. I think the second one is words of affirmation. In my eyes she is just adorable and beautiful. When I tell her that, she will say, "Mom you are seeing me through eyes of love," and I say of course I am, but it's true also! My oldest son, Adam, seems to need acts of service and words of affirmation. My youngest one, Richard, needs words of affirmation. I tend to give acts of service to my sons as well as quality time because I think those were the two that my parents most demanded, and remember, we model on our parents. So I will bake cookies, do laundry, run some of my sons' errands, buy fish food for Richard's fish, and things like that to show I care. While I am not big for getting gifts and I think that is a lesser preferred language for most people, I love to give gifts to others. Maybe for me that is another example of acts of service. But before I learned all this and put it to work I had an incident that shocked me. One day Richard complained and felt very hurt that I never complimented his work at school and how hard he works. I felt I had but it was not enough to meet his need. He was really hurt by that lack of love as he saw it. He really didn't see my appreciative gestures in acts of service as a meaningful act of love. Now we could have had a fight over who was the most underappreciated but fighting solves nothing. If we remember that anger, according to Dr. Phil, is hurt, fear, or frustration, we can see that we are hurt in this sort of situation. Given all my practice seeing this, I quickly apologized and explained the five languages of love. I promised to work harder to provide what he needed. But given that I just love to give acts of service, I made a decision to help translate for him. When I baked cookies for him, I would ask, "I did that why?" At first he was a bit surprised at the question. Then I quickly said, "Because I love you!" That would get a teenage blush. But once he got used to the question, he would respond that it was because I loved him. So I changed it up to say, "No, because I love you better than any other teen in the universe!" It gets a laugh and gets the point across while I am also using my language of love and his.

I have found that if you become sensitive to what you want in the language of love, you make better choices in the relationships you have, no matter if they are romantic or just friendships. Life is very much colored by the quality of your relationships, and what is better than making sure you are getting and delivering the emotional nutritional needs of those you love? We are developing an adult friendship and special bond with our young adult. If there is a lot of strife in a house where there is frustration over the young adult not becoming independent, there will be a lot of back messages as to their worth and a lot fear and frustration on the parents' part that they haven't done a good job launching their child. As the Dog Whisperer, Cesar Millan teaches that we want to be calm and assertive leaders. We also want to be nurturing parents not Drill Sergeant or Helicopter parents.

We have discussed tools now that will help you tailor a plan for your young adult. In the past, just as marriages were arranged, careers were planned without regard to the person or their personality. I will never forget how Harold's mother once told me that she and her husband had decided that Harold would become a doctor and his brother would be a dentist. They liked these professions for their security and status. They told my sons that Richard should be an accountant and Adam should be a lawyer. They have quietly pushed these *dreams* onto their grandsons and are somewhat frustrated that they aren't taking. Howard, their son, did become a doctor, but he would have preferred a different profession. His brother pursued sales and became a multi-millionaire who loved owning his own planes and flying. A dentist's life wouldn't have worked for him. It would have been way too confining and boring. Being a lawyer myself, I wouldn't mind if one of my sons was a lawyer. However, that isn't the personality of either one of my sons. That isn't who they are and I want them to be happy finding out what their lives are about and where they will be most fulfilled. Remember, your need for security isn't about them. With love and support, they will find their way and once they do find it they will settle into a security also. If people aren't happy they won't settle in and be emotionally secure, even if they are financially secure.

So let's move into some concrete work in launching. From our previous work you understand better now the changes going on within your young adult and have adjusted your expectations to be more realistic about how much they can handle. You are working on listening to your young adult and getting to know them. You are becoming a good coach. You can't put together a winning team without knowing the strengths and weaknesses of your players and that you are learning. I hope you are also being kind to yourself. You didn't have tools before. It is a new era for all of you. We are beginning today. Since much of the foundation for the young adult happens in the teen years, and many of you still have teens to parent, let's start with what a teen needs skill-wise to transition into adulthood. If these skills are missing in your young adult, make them a priority. It is never too late. ✄

Chapter 10 Skills My Teen Needs to Have

Now we are getting down to the nitty-gritty of the parenting work we need to do! As I said, we start to go wrong on parenting in the teen years. Let's assume we are now committed to a more positive parenting approach. What do we do?

We need to think of adulthood like we think of school or college. If you go to middle school, high school, or college, you have to take some classes like math, science, and English as basics. Then you get to have some choices that suit your interests such as music, a language, drama, and the like. In short, you are building skills to move you forward in your education. For some reason, parents today seem to think these things can be accomplished by teens on their own. In fact, they often get angry that their teens aren't becoming helpful, appreciative, productive members of the family and society. We are failing them. Our expectations are wrong and as parents we aren't giving them the basics, so that's where we will start. What does an enabled teen coming out of high school need in terms of the basics? Here is my list and where I try to steer parents.

The Basics List

1. A driver's license, at least by age 18.

2. A job or a series of jobs, paid or unpaid, such as internships.

3. A savings account.

4. Lessons in bill paying, budgeting, and money management.

5. Lesson in cooking, laundry, sewing, car and home maintenance.

6. Lessons in room cleanliness.

The Extras

1. A passport

2. Volunteer work

3. Investment education

4. Vacations and time together

It is amazing how few teens today graduate high school with the life skills needed on this list. Some of you will think they are just not that important but let me explain what we are looking for in each one of them.

A Driver's License, At Least By Age 18

I have taught several young adults how to drive. My oldest son, Adam, wanted to get his driver's license right away, at the earliest possible moment. Richard wasn't too far behind when he hit 15 and a half, the earliest you can get your driver's permit and start driving. I had been the same because to me as a teenager it meant freedom to go places. However, I noticed some teens in my sons' age group were reluctant and overwhelmed by the paperwork process. Dealing with any unknown system does that to all of us. In this day and age, I find systems and organizations changing at a heady rate. Some of it is due to the computer age, but some is just that as new people come into an organization, new methods and ideas take hold quickly. Unfortunately, they usually have defects that need to be ironed out. This takes feedback, patience, and learning to find someone in the system that can affect change. We all need to learn to self teach our way through other people's systems. Helping your teen to do this is critical to teaching them how to start dealing with the real world. This will be one of their first times to be treated as an adult or almost as an adult. Even in the few years between when my sons got their licenses until Justin got his, I noticed that things changed in the system for obtaining a license. What I think many in our generation and certainly in our parents' generation find to be hard is learning to ask questions and figure out things on our own. In the past, in a much more authoritarian society, things got done a certain way, you were informed, and you followed the rules. You didn't ask to bend rules or work outside of the system. Today, rules and methods change all the time. You have to have built in flexibility. Some of us in the baby boomer generation and younger generations have learned to do research and become informed consumers. But there is still a large number of people who are afraid to ask questions that let us know what the process and procedure is in each system. It is important to model this behavior for our young adults.

Some teens aren't emotionally ready and need a little time to see how things are playing out with their peers in terms of getting a license. They have to figure out if they want a license, if it looks doable for them, or if can they wait. In almost all of these new situations, there is a lot of transition anxiety. We have to remember that they have been children following someone else's orders and demands. That is still how most schools are run. What we are asking now is that they develop a sense of decision making and exercise their own judgment and problem solving abilities. In short they have to learn to fly and they aren't piggybacked onto another adult now. This is a really big transition. It is here that I have to remind parents that what is now easy for us is not yet easy for them. But you can't let them get too afraid to ever tackle the situation or postpone it too long. Once a certain level of fear sets in, it demoralizes them and brings down their self-esteem. As other friends get their licenses, they look like failures.

I was told by one dad that his daughter loved having him chauffeur her around. This was a dad who loved spending time with his children and it was a great bonding experience for him. While it was generally nice to think about being so needed and appreciated, I seriously doubt she felt that way all of the time. After all, it leaves her

Chapter 10 Skills My Teen Needs to Have

dependent on his availability and it doesn't look good to her peer group. It is a child's status, not an emerging adult's status. My advice is to get the license but have just one car if dad wants to keep chauffeuring her. She needs this skill and she needs to stand up tall with her peers. I have seen teens just get the license but not drive much. It never lasts long, but it is important to get the license. Teens that hit 18 without getting their licenses start to feel ashamed. I've heard all the excuses but the bottom line is that they know that they don't measure up to their peers. It also leaves them vulnerable to situations. One reason I was teaching 20-year-old Cindy to drive was that her single mother had an accident and broke her arm. Cindy was unavailable to help her mother because she couldn't drive. At college, Cindy was one of few who didn't drink at parties, which made her the ideal designated driver. But she had to get in cars with people who may have had a drink or two because she couldn't drive.

It also limits a lot of their job opportunities. Without a car, you must focus on how easy it is to get to and from work. When Justin and I were looking for jobs for him at a nearby airport, several required a driver's license for various jobs. You could hear the shame in his voice when he realized that was a qualification he couldn't fulfill. I have had other parents say that when their teens want to work they are limited to places that the teen can get to by public transportation. Driving is a critical aspect of being an adult. Also, once you have a license, you are dealing with many other adult situations. You have to have insurance, current registration, a good mechanic, and you get to wash and maintain a car. These are all new areas to manage and deal with at an adult level. I still feel that even if you plan to never drive again, at least get a license. It is an important skill and you will not be vulnerable to finding rides and limiting possible job or career opportunities.

I have seen parents leave this up to their adult child time and time again. The idea is that they need to step up to the plate and be responsible. That makes sense once you know how to handle the responsibility, but this is new to them. They are going from following orders to being in a position of authority. Yet, these transitions aren't across the board. They are in a position of authority in one area but not in another. In school, they still have to follow very strict rules without much flexibility. If they are too overwhelmed to go deal with this initial transition then go with them. Go with them to get their license even if you have to make the appointment. If you are too afraid to teach them how to drive and a lot of people are, then find an adult or relative who will. Cindy was a petrified driving student starting out but we had her license in six weeks and about 20-30 hours of driving. As I told her over and over, it is a skill. Among the aspects of the skill set is the ability to have a map in your mind of where to go and how to get there, learning how to follow directions, how to work the car, how to understand other drivers and what they are going to do while actively remembering the rules of the road. In time, it gets easier. It was wonderful to watch her confidence grow and, as with Justin, she wondered why she hadn't done it sooner. Fear needs to be mastered along with the adult skill involved. This is important. Fear keeps so many of us from attempting the next hurdle. Everything has a learning curve and mistakes will be made. So many of us see the mistakes we make as we learn new skills as a failure in who we are, thus making us less worthwhile, less valuable. Your teen and young adult will see that also, as they live in a social structure that is brutal in judging them. As I have told all my driving students, if you don't pass the written test on the first try, keep taking it. Eventually, you will pass. That is same for the road test. Then if you never want to drive again, fine but at least you can if you need to or want to drive. The same goes for when teens go to college their first year and having cars on campus is discouraged. Don't leave your young adult without this skill even if they don't have car. At least they can drive their friends home from parties and they aren't left vulnerable.

A Job or A Series Of Jobs, Paid or Unpaid, Such As Internship

By age 14 or 15, your teenager needs to be working. Babysitting, doing lawn work, and cleaning houses are fine for 12- to 15-year-old entrepreneurs, but once in high school, they need to be in a more structured work situation. At that point the teen needs to learn the work ethic that requires they follow rules and answer to a boss. They need to learn the responsibilities that come with a job such as how to dress, how to interact with co-workers and the public, and how to be on time and manage money. This is also the start to figuring out what they might want to do as a career. Along with this it doesn't hurt to start a savings account and learn the ins and outs of banking. The management of time and money is the hardest for most young adults and sometimes for older adults. This is a good starting point to some very adult responsibilities. Furthermore, it builds a work resume and garners recommendations from bosses and co-workers which is another important skill. Teens who aren't working are either getting into trouble or are so studious that they find this very hard to deal with once their lives as students are done. Both are at serious disadvantages in the work world if they don't start early. Do not sacrifice this skill building for academics only. This is a huge mistake many parents make. The assumption that kids walk into work with only a college degree and do well is laughable, but that is happening in most situations. In fact, I just had a number of friends with 22-year-old students graduating college. Some came from the best schools and almost all had not worked very much if at all in their lives. They are having trouble finding work and what they do find they can't live on very well. Why? No one wants to hire a person who has never proven they are a good worker. To an employer, a degree is worthless. It means you can study. It does not mean you can work.

When they start working, teens start to feel like adults. They are beginning to have adult confidence and they are beginning to understand work politics and dynamics. They experience the dynamics of paying taxes, maybe filing for a tax refund, and feeling a bit more involved with what happens to the taxes they are paying. This has a lot of repercussions beyond just earning a little money. How we got away from these values and skills is sad. But the good news is that it is very easy to fix.

I have heard parents say there are no jobs for teens. I call that *not looking*. There are restaurant jobs, small store jobs, park and recreation center jobs, daycare assisting, bookstore jobs, pet store jobs, and on and on. Do they pay a lot? Not usually. They may not pay at all initially, but find a small local newspaper or look in the Help Wanted section. One of the best ways to find jobs is through networking, family and friends who may have leads. This has been a time honored tradition and what they will need to use when they graduate. They need to learn to network in their teen years. Have your student go online to www.craigslist.com or some other website that lists jobs. The idea is to learn to get your foot in the door of somewhere you want to work and gives the parent an idea of what sorts of jobs or careers your teen or young adult is interested in. Remember, this is the start of a lot of skill sets. Looking for work is a skill set and getting the job and working is another skill set. I discourage parents who

Chapter 10 Skills My Teen Needs to Have

have businesses from hiring their teens as those parents give their teens breaks in schedules and maybe in the work place. They need to learn to work with others, answer to others, and earn the respect of others. It also helps them develop their own identity away from you and this is important. You want your teen to become independent, that means on their own and dealing with bosses and coworkers where they may not get preferential treatment. If they want to come work for you later on after other jobs, that is fine, but they need to go get a sense of their own work ethic under normal, not preferential conditions. This is all about building skills and confidence in the real world.

Many of us do know friends or have connections to others who may have jobs for our teens and that is fine. I have seen that work out many times because the teen also knows that their behavior will be reported back to you, good and bad. During the school year, keep it reasonable, say around eight hours or less, depending on the other responsibilities. Help your student reflect on the job in terms of how it fits him or her. I have offered at times to pay my sons if they want to try unpaid internships in areas they might want to explore for a possible career. The point is that they still have a schedule and a boss to report to as well as doing the work. An unpaid internship is also a way to get into a job in that company or business later on as people learn the quality of their work. Some people think that internships don't get counted as jobs that you have had. They do and are a good way to start building experience. Keep in mind that is job exploration and if a job isn't working out, it is fine to let it go as long as there is movement toward another job.

One parent complained that her son simply quit his job and was now sitting on the couch doing nothing following high school graduation. Make it clear to your teen or young adult that the way to leave one job that isn't working is to have another one lined up and give the proper notice. This also leads to the job skill of the proper exit. Sometimes, people are so upset with the job they are leaving that they want to go out in a blaze of glory by telling off the people who have offended them. This is called *burning bridges* and it's not a good thing to do. What feels good at the moment doesn't take into account that over time, management changes. Bosses move on, perhaps co-workers move up into management. If someone left with a lot of bad blood in the company there is a long enough memory not to want a previous worker to return. Many companies will take you back in a management or higher position once you have added experience elsewhere or college classes in the career field. As much as you might want to have your say, suppress it. Things change. This is a skill your young adult needs.

Underlying the job world is the need for a social security number if they haven't already gotten one. All of these skills have a number of aspects that need to be addressed. Social security numbers can be gotten when your child is an infant as there is no age requirement. We who are older have forgotten how overwhelming all these details can be. They entail figuring out where to go, what is needed, who to talk to, and what steps should be taken. But a social security number should be obtained first, even if they are in an unpaid internship. You want things in place as you go through transitions because there are so many transitions to go through in this phase of child development.

93

Another aspect to finding work that young people don't understand is that you are building your pay scale. If you start at $8/hr. for this job, at the next you will want to require more pay, say up to $10/hr. Today's college graduates don't understand this. They feel their degree dictates the higher pay they have heard you could get in that career. If you never had a paying job, guess where you start on the pay scale? You start at the bottom. Most college students don't understand working up the ladder of pay and responsibility and they don't understand changing jobs to promote your career. Even sadder, they don't understand what pay scales make up their fields of interest. Discouraged and humiliated to be going nowhere with their degrees they take lower pay and assume that is all they are worth. This is the biggest problem with today's teens and young adults; they don't have a real sense of working and a career.

A Savings Account

When I was a teen, I had a savings account for the income from my summer jobs. I think today that it is even more important. Being a minor, I had to have my mother set it up, but I had access to it. There is so much more to learn today than there was back then. Today there is the convenience of online banking with online bill pay, automatic deposit and withdrawal, and convenient 24 hour ATM. With all of these comes the potential for problems. It is important to learn how to be safe in whom you allow access to your account, and that especially means businesses.

Justin had been living on his own for his last year of high school. His parents were going through a messy divorce and he was 18. His aunt had set him up in his own apartment so that he didn't have to move and could finish out his senior year. This was a horrible year for him. He was still working part-time and juggling the demands of living alone, cooking, cleaning, and laundry on top of school and it was too much at times. A salesman came to his door selling magazine subscriptions. Even I have fallen for the smooth and convincing talk and Justin was no match for them. Lonely and enjoying the attention, he signed up for a number of magazines for several years. When he was living with me, he was still getting them some two years after he initially signed up for them. Although he e-mailed and called them to cancel, their promises to do so went ignored and he continued to have money deducted from his account on a regular basis because he had let them do automatic payment withdrawal. I helped write a letter and he closed his account so that they could no longer do the automatic withdrawals. In that time, he lost a lot of money that could have been spent on other things. Rather than allow that, it is best to do bill paying through your bank. You do the paying and the company does not have free access to take from your account.

Perhaps some of you are not computer savvy with these sorts of online banking systems. They are very easy to set up and use. However, if you are intimidated you can take your young adult into the bank to talk to an accounts manager and they can get them set up to do online banking. Teach them to get to know their banking representatives. As much as you can, teach them how to be wise about a number of these things. There is a lot of fraud out in the real world. In the world of e-mail there are phishers who pose as some sort of legitimate company, complete with their logos and such, pretending to need you to confirm your account. Unsuspecting people disclose valuable information that allows these frauds to access their accounts or create identity theft. If contacted by phone or e-mail, do not give out account

Chapter 10 Skills My Teen Needs to Have

information. I've tried to train my sons about the various ways scam artists work and to be suspicious.

Recently, Adam was contacted by a gym I belong to. They said that someone sent an e-mail stating they were him and they were requesting information on joining the gym. The odd part was they had his old college address, cell phone number, and his e-mail was off by one digit. The woman claimed that the gym had been getting some strange e-mails from out of the country and so they were suspicious enough to try to verify identity. First I gave Adam the number of the gym and told him to call back. Some scam artists will give you the number they are calling from so that if you call back, they answer with the false name of the company, leading you to believe you have reached the right company. Finding the correct phone number from your bills or other ways independent of the potential scammer is important.

Secondly, we tried to figure out what it was the scammer was trying to acquire. My son has a different last name from mine so there was no way they could access my account information nor did my name come up. He didn't have an account there so they couldn't access any identity information on him. Opening a gym membership in his name wouldn't net them much of anything as far as we could tell so the angle of why this was being done eluded us. We discussed if maybe this was some sort of prank by someone mad at him. Were they hoping that the bill for membership would be forwarded from his old address to his present one and then he'd have the hassle of disavowing any knowledge? But they'd have to sign a contract and all of this seemed like a lot of work for some benefit we couldn't guess at. It did provide us with a lot of conversation and learning to tease out the scam and whether there was some sort of identity theft going on. He did call the gym and got the woman who contacted him again so we knew that was legitimate. It also inspired me to get identity theft protection for all of us. We realized that the problems successful theft could cause were so bad to contemplate that the few dollars a month were worth it.

When I was growing up, my parents didn't discuss their finances or money management with us kids. It was considered very private and inappropriate for us to know. That may still be the case for most families. However, Robert Kiyosaki in *Rich Dad, Poor Dad,* as I recall, said that it was talking about money and learning about money management that works best for all of us. I think he is right. I was so naïve out on my own at age 18. I have tried to teach my sons and Justin how to ask questions, how to take time to make decisions after reaching money management issues. Remembering that their brains are still growing, there will be certain impulsiveness to spending it and managing it. Preparing for future needs by saving money and such is still a foreign concept because they are still in the teen and young adult belief that bad things don't happen to them but only to others. Personal finances today can be so tricky that it is important to let them start managing money and even paying bills through you like cell phones or car insurance. It isn't long before they have to do it on their own.

When I sold our family home to downsize since I had two sons off to college, I included my sons in as many of the meetings with realtors and tax attorneys and the like so that they not only knew my finances but also became comfortable with the process of dealing with money. I had been so afraid of dealing with big money deals as a young adult that I never bought a car until I was in my 40's. I let husbands do that sort of thing. Even buying a home I left to my father-in-law and husband. Yet I was an attorney who wasn't afraid to handle all those transactions for others. Money management on a personal level frightened me in part because it frightened my parents who had so little with which to raise a large family. Once I began the process of doing it, I regretted missed opportunities and a life-style that would have looked different and been more suited to me.

When I was 19 and putting myself through college, I had joined a karate school to learn how to defend myself, being a young woman alone in the world. The owner of the school must have seen how naïve I was. He also saw how much I loved karate. He approached me and said he was looking for people to purchase a lifetime membership. I have forgotten how much it was. Maybe it was a few thousand dollars, so, compared to college, it didn't look bad, but for a girl on her own, it was a lot in day-to-day expenses. I explained I didn't have that money. I was working part-time and he suggested I go to my credit union and borrow it. I even needed a co-signer and how I talked a fellow worker into co-signing I will never know. But I did and got the membership and felt like I had been helpful and important for having such a membership. I barely found time to take classes over the next few years and by age 21 got married and moved out of state. Had I known how much young people move around and how quickly they lose interest, I would have put that money toward a used car. I am amazed at some of my dumb decisions. I can't save my sons from bad decisions; they will make a few, but hopefully a lot less than I did, using reasoned judgment, not ignorance. I enjoy teaching my sons and other young adults how to negotiate, how to research, how to weigh options of purchases and other money deals now. You can't save them from mistakes but you can try to minimize mistakes through some sort of education.

Money is an emotional issue. How people manage and spend it varies widely. Many parents worry that their young adults aren't spending wisely and saving for the future. These are all prudent ideas, of course, from years of experience. But you can't intellectually graft your experience onto others. They are going to have to learn for themselves, as frustrating as that is for us who have to stand back and watch. The best skill we can impart here is to make sure that they look at options and weigh them. If they are making a purchase of a car or home, you can only make sure that they have done their homework and made sure that they are getting the best deal. Beyond that, what they chose to spend their money on is an emotional issue that you can't control, nor should you. It is their life and they have to learn to make those decisions.

I know one man who was becoming very successful after years of working hard. Charles told me one day while we were chatting that he found himself spending like he had never done before and it worried him. He just enjoyed buying things that he had to pass over before. Even with Justin, I noticed that he had a tendency to buy a ton of clothes once he was making money. I had done the same when I was first married and we began to have a professional income. Like Justin and Charles, finally being able to expand into someone new who could buy things was like freedom. Justin and I grew up poor. We were almost afraid to go into high-end stores for fear our income status would be challenged and we'd be thrown out as imposters and identified as the poor people we saw ourselves as being. I gave my sons allowances when they were in elementary school and their reaction was the same. A heady sense of freedom to indulge one's immediate wishes took hold and the money was gone. The lesson I taught them then was no more buying until the next week. That seemed harsh but they learned to look for bargains and to wait on purchases. In some ways, emerging young adults have the same impulses. Once again we have to understand they are going from emotional centered thinking in the brain to developing the brain connections that give them better judgment. When I hear parents complain, I have to explain, their children are learning and they will have different life priorities than us. A nice car has emotional meaning and social value whereas we older adults have long since cared little for impressing our friends. At least, many of us have moved on, but some have not.

It isn't just having a savings account that matters, it is teaching your young adult money management early, letting them learn to handle it, and teaching them to be smart and cautious consumers.

Lessons In Bill Paying, Budgeting, And Money Management

We already discussed how to help your teen or young adult learn to deal with a banking system and online banking. However, it is very important to get your teens and younger kids paying for things early on. As I said with my sons, they bought their own extra toys with an allowance. Some of that but by no means all was their *job*. I have had more than one client contact me that their young adult has finished college and had a job but quit it and now does nothing but hang out with friends. This is a very common scenario. In one case, the father had given the son a second car to use but all that the son paid for was gas. As we worked out the game plan for his independence, top on the list was that it was time for him to pay for room and board and car insurance at the very least. Paying for his own clothes and paying for his entertainment were also on the list. Even though he didn't have job yet, he needed to have bills to start letting him know what sort of salary he needed. The mother said he had done a good job of getting a part-time pizza restaurant job. I said that is unacceptable. Mostly because it was only part-time and wouldn't cover much of any of his bills, this left him in the position of being dependent. He wasn't job hunting very hard. The pizza job only came up because after living at home for a number of months, she had given him a deadline to get out and it was coming up fast. He needed either two part-time jobs or one better paying full-time job. This is why I emphasize, that starting your working life upon college graduation is a bad idea. One friend told me of another friend whose son had finished college with a ton of student loans. The entry-level job he was getting would never start to pay them off and he could look at finally paying them off in middle age! This is becoming more and more the norm. As consumers of education, we aren't planning it or understanding it very well. I'll give some tips later on about how to reduce the cost of a 4-year degree.

Getting a job needs a context and that context is the lifestyle you want or hope to have down the line in life. Our pizza guy wasn't seeing a job as a means to fulfill responsibilities. When they had the meeting, he got very upset to find out he was going to have to pay for room and board. Yet out on his own, this would be a reality he would have to deal with. When Justin moved out on his own after living with us it was to a room in the home of a single mother. It was cheaper than having a studio apartment and he didn't have to set up utility accounts and the like, which sometimes require deposits for young people who haven't established credit. It doesn't hurt to take your young adult around to look at places to get ideas of just what things will cost and how much you get for various prices. If you are short on time, look through the online rentals or rentals in local newspapers. It isn't until they have a real sense of the cost of being independent that the wheels in their heads start to move as to what it will take job-wise and career-wise. It is also important to lay down the idea that they should aspire to having the home of their dreams and start thinking of what will get them there one day.

I had one mother who was very disappointed that her son went to work rather than stay home and do college. Within a year of being on his own he encountered roommate problems. Living with roommates is a great way to gather a number of life skills. You have to learn to choose the right living situation, learn to apportion bills, share chores, share items, and resolve conflicts. My oldest son, Adam, is a fairly neat person. When he went off to his first year of college, one of the dorm questionnaire questions addressed how neat you wanted your roommate to be. Luckily he and Cody both wanted fairly neat roommates and it worked out well for them. When he transferred to another school several years later, he decided to live with one of his good friends and a third guy in an apartment. Despite being really compatible friends in most of life, their neatness standards were very different. It chipped away at the relationship and he commented when he moved to transfer again a year later that he would never live with him again as much as he liked the guy. As I tried to tell the mom, having roommate issues isn't a bad thing. It teaches you a lot. More than likely one day you will settle down to marry. Love is great but day-to-day habits count a lot in your ongoing happiness.

The balance you want is that your teen and young adult learns to manage bills and financial responsibilities with buying *luxury* items. Keep in mind that this may take years for them to learn. Buying, like alcohol or sex, can be a stress reliever and like other *addictions* or self-comforting habits, they may get out of hand from time to time. Make allowances for a few mistakes. I know at some point almost every parent is asked or offers to help with a financial glitch. The key is not to let it become a pattern. That becomes the road to enabling and dependence. If these missteps are happening more than two or three times in a two to three year period, there has to be a serious conversation about money management. Not everyone is good at seeing what they are doing and making better decisions. If you do have a need to point it out, be non-judgmental and realize that there are different approaches.

In one of my marriages, my father-in-law decided he was going to have us set up retirement accounts and college accounts for the future as he had done in his family. It had worked well in his marriage and he was going to manage it for us the same way and spare us the work he had gone through. This is a common problem that parents have. We still want to protect and short cut the whole process that life skills take. Living is fraught with learning and enduring many ups and downs. We would love our children to benefit from our experiences and mistakes and then just live life with few worries and hassles. But that isn't how parenting works. Everyone has the right to create the life they want and often it means just learning what it is that we want. We need to make the mistakes and find our strengths and weaknesses and what makes us smile and reduce our stresses. It is our job to create our own lives. In my marriage, things went horribly wrong with this imposed benevolence. My father-in-law didn't have the same priorities in spending and saving we had, and our professions had gone

Chapter 10 Skills My Teen Needs to Have

into major transitions with less disposable income. We couldn't afford his plans but he wouldn't hear of it. It tore us apart trying to please him and live our lives. You have to let your young adult make his or her purchases, mistakes, or indulgences. It is their life. It is only when they want you to have the burden of paying for their choices that you get to have a comment and the greatest gift you can give is firm kindness. Remember as in all else, work the problem, not the kid.

It is a good idea to teach your teen and young adult how to make a budget. Sometimes, unless you write it down, you don't realize where the money is going. When my youngest son was getting ready to go off to college, his father asked him to come up with a budget for funds that his father would dispense from the college fund. For weeks, nothing happened. It was becoming a point of contention between the two of them. Knowing young people, I realize when I am getting non-compliance or resistance, as they frequently don't know how to tackle the issue. I asked my son if he knew how to make a budget. As with so many life skills, parents assume the skill already exists and the child is just being lazy. Too frequently, the skill isn't there and the young adult is too embarrassed to ask for help. As it turned out, my son didn't have the foggiest idea how to make a budget. So we sat down together and had a conversation. Never having been out on his own, there were things he didn't know yet that would be a part of that budget. He already paid bills for his car and entertainment and his clothes, but he didn't know about textbooks, food, laundry, and other needs. It gave us a chance to talk about going off to college and what life in the dorm would be like. We also consulted his older brother to see if there were things we forgot. Things are different today from when I went to college. We didn't have phone and cable bills to consider. I also found that since the boys had been handling some bills, they were fairly conservative in spending money. When young people handle money they begin to get the value of it and the cost to others to provide it. Budgeting is an excellent life skill. Start it early if possible. Budgeting and managing some bills, be it spending an allowance for toys, games, or gas early on, are the steps you want your teens and young adults to be skilled in for their independence. Don't forget that they will make mistakes; they will need some help for the surprises that life brings. That is when they start to understand having funds put aside for those unexpected events. They don't know that until they go through it the first few times.

Lessons In Cooking, Laundry, Sewing, Car and Home Maintenance

I think of this as part of stress management, the same as teaching them to exercise. Any older person will tell you that health is everything. Without it the quality of life is so much diminished. As obesity is on the rise, it is critical to counter it with healthy exercise and eating. Both of my sons took cooking classes in middle school. In fact, back in the day when I was in middle school, girls took cooking, guys took woodwork. Now both sexes take both if it is offered. My sons enjoyed cooking and baking. Our own fare at home came from my trying to avoid the cooking I grew up with. I came from the Midwest, where the food was commonly heavily laden with creams, fat, and fried with bacon grease. I hear that similar eating happens in the South. What was missing were fresh fruits and vegetables. My mother used canned or frozen vegetables and salads were rare. Some of these traditions came from the fact that in an agrarian society, the work of farming burned off so many calories that you needed lots of calories for energy. Cooked food protected against bacteria and other contaminants.

99

Moving to California, I learned to make more fresh foods that have the vitamins and minerals that we need.

While my sons love to eat fresh, it is easy but expensive to get already made foods at upscale supermarkets. I have bought them George Forman's grill and snack makers for college because they want things fast. I have discovered that the thing they don't understand about food preparation is that a lot of work goes into shopping and planning for meals, followed by the actual preparation, cooking, and clean up time. There is also learning to make enough for leftovers, which are convenient and often more flavorful over time. Young people tend to think in the immediate. But when you cook a meal every day, it is time consuming. Having leftovers or food that can be turned into a second meal is good planning and less time consuming. Shopping and learning to have staples is something they don't understand. Don't forget they are learning time management and for those who never cooked meals while they were in high school, it looks easy. Now juggling studies or a job and everything else, it takes a large chunk of time out of a day. If there is one thing I want parents to understand in all these life skills it is that it is a balancing act of resources that we do more easily because of practice. They haven't had practice by and large, and we've neglected to teach them.

If you cook at home, it is also a great activity to bond over. I'm not just advocating life skills to launch your teen or young adult; I'm trying to get you to have a new adult-to-adult relationship that is close and supportive of one another. Bonding happens especially well while doing tasks together. Before we were an industrial society, women learned from their mothers and close female relatives how to cook, clean, do laundry, and run a family and a home. Men also learned to work the farm or where trades were involved, they apprenticed. Role modeling is so important and has such a strong impact on who the young adult becomes. Parenting as a mentorship at this stage of life can be fun and rewarding. It also helps to pass the torch to the next generation. In so many of my consultations, I hear angst in the voice of the parents. Their young are breaking away in many respects. The empty nest syndrome looms over them. This can become a bit easier when there has been some attempt at a new supportive role and through role modeling. You are still needed, but in a different capacity than as one who does everything for them and saves them from life's difficulties.

Any of these sorts of household skills that you can share are great. I've taught my sons to iron and sew buttons on a shirt. My oldest son loves to have a fresh pressed look and has gotten good at ironing even when I'd let something go. My youngest son has forgotten how to sew on a button, so we do it again. As with any skill, if you have done it once, you know you can do it again. Adding water to the car radiator, checking the oil in the car, and all those car maintenance things are essential. Learning to change the furnace filter, or cleaning out gutters, or whatever household chores you can impart, tells them that they can do it and they too will be steward of the property they own. It builds respect for you when they do it as they didn't know the behind the scenes responsibilities hefted upon us and it builds respect for them as they take on new adult skills and responsibilities. Think over what you can share with them and have them help you with around the house. Most of my siblings and I clearly remember these moments growing up. It is a part of growing up and leaving childhood behind. Perhaps for you, it helps you to get used to seeing things that way also.

Chapter 10 Skills My Teen Needs to Have

Lessons In Room Cleanliness

You may wonder why this is even in here along with all the other sorts of doing chore pages. These all relate to life skills, respecting others, and being respected. Most of us, whether we have gone to college or gone from home out into the work world, start out with roommates. Entry level jobs seldom allow teens to have their own apartments, so like Justin, they may have a room in a boarding situation, or like my college aged sons, they may have roommates, so household chores and getting along become critical. Even my lovely daughter in living with her fiancé finds it a challenge deciding who is going to do what chores. Marriages present the same issues. When you live with someone, you must resolve the issues of standards of neatness and who is to do which chores. Roommate problems frequently arise because of conflicts around these issues. This is also a secondary opportunity to show how to resolve these conflicts. The more skills you can give your young adult in these areas, the better. After all, conflict resolution is critical for work and for life in general.

I am on a panel of parenting experts and we once received a question from a mother about how to get her elementary school aged children to pick up their toys more consistently. As with all parenting, you have to get your expectations to reasonable levels instead of perfection levels. We all have things slip from time to time. Perfection is not a livable state and is usually imposed as a way to be abusive and controlling. It has little to do with the failure and much to do with the person imposing the standard. When my sons were younger, I would say to them that I know it is my issue but I need the house to be fairly mess free, especially if I didn't make the mess. I asked them to do it to help me. This goes back to boundaries and imposing your limits on others. Be reasonable and if you are hearing that you aren't, own the fact that maybe for greater neatness, you need to do more of the work. In the law, we talk of "reasonable man standards" in regards to judging. We all know people with less than high standards in cleanliness and neatness but we also know people who are compulsive in their order and standards. The key is to be in the middle.

Most people seem to feel that children should be able to help pick up after themselves in the elementary school years. I have heard that if the habit hasn't been formed early on, there is going to be nothing but parental frustration for middle school and high school aged children's messiness. It isn't a lost cause even then. It is a habit. The goal isn't to get frustrated, angry, or demanding, but rather to instill a habit. In my family, after trying to find homework or other needed items in my son's room, I instituted a need for order. If I was going to be put to the effort of last minute searching for items, it only seemed fair to have some order from which to operate. Jo Frost, the expert nanny in the TV show *Supernanny*, has a number of tricks for getting little ones to cooperate in cleaning up and picking up and doing chores. Everything from bonus boards of earning a special treat to merely praising and helping them. When I instituted some sense of order with my older son, he was about eight years old. Up until then I did a lot of the clean up. I would help him at the end of the day, and as he got older I would ask him to do it before we went on a fun outing. If he needed help, I helped. When you get delays or excuses, then a good way to get past the inertia is to go in and help. As they get older, they are not so crazy about *help*.

When Justin moved in with us, I asked him to keep some order in his room. He had never really learned as his mother was lost in her drinking too frequently and he was

101

busy helping raise his sister or working part-time. I had to do a lot of reminding. It just wasn't a habit for him. I also had to lower my standards. It would take a long time to get that sort of habit. Ironically, when he moved in with the landlady and her two sons and another boarder, he had to adhere to the same standard of neatness in common areas. Within a year when he had me see a new computer in his room, I was shocked. The invitation into the room was spur of the moment so it wasn't as if he had cleaned up for entertaining, but it was very orderly. It takes time to develop habits and they aren't nearly as embraced if someone is beating you over the head. When he went back to the Midwest to visit his mother that summer he came back shocked that he could no longer tolerate the mess and disorder in his mother's home.

Am I claiming this as a virtue for everyone? No. It makes life easier as my friend, Jackie, a professional organizer would tell you. Once you are lost in chaos at home, it is hard to live your work life and personal life. Neatness just makes it easier to get along with roommates and significant others. It is another life skill. Adam, my oldest son, looks for roommates who are similarly neat. Adam tells me that it is hard for him to keep track of things if he isn't organized, so he makes it a priority. He and other roommates have asked a messy roommate to move out simply because they were finding it hard to pick up after the messy roommate. Even when the mess maker tried to make amends, he just couldn't sustain neatness or help with chores for more than a few days. His habit was so ingrained that even at the cost of moving, he couldn't break it fast enough. I have parents asking me how to get their teen or young adult to change, especially once the young adult is 18 or older and doesn't feel that they have to follow standards. Let's talk about his briefly.

When you want an adult's cooperation, you have to ask nicely and explain it. Find out if they feel the chore is doable. What you want is for them to buy into the cooperation. Ask them what they think a consequence should be if they don't come through. I am not saying to use a punishment like when they were little children, but perhaps a task you do for them isn't done such as food bought or cooked or laundry done for them. Have a discussion on how often the chore should be done and ask if there is something you can do for them to foster a sense of cooperation. Parents often give orders; they don't ask and they don't talk about it. You are negotiating for a certain behavior so you have to talk about it and you have to present what it is you are giving in exchange. You may already be giving them things so you need to make clear that it is part of the give and take. Many times young people feel that you are not giving something back in return because they still want to assume the child status. One parent was giving her 18-year-old son gas money in sympathy for the high cost of gas and his still low paying job. These are still children in terms of brain function. Gently refuse. It is best to work out this give and take in advance of conflict. The parent in this example needs to say there are only two choices; get a second job to pay for gas or do the chores on a weekly basis and earn gas money from the parent. We are drawing boundaries now for respecting the parent as an adult and not just as a parent anymore. The same goes for rent and other costly items in that you need to put these things on the table as things to be earned if they want to be treated as young adults. You have to work out give and take. It is all too easy for them to revert back to a child/parent relationship when they don't want responsibility and then to an adult/adult relationship when they want privileges. It has to be discussed and negotiated in a calm, thoughtful manner in a meeting. It doesn't hurt to revisit the situation and refine your agreement.

Parents sometimes feel bad that since the room is technically their child's, and especially if the young adult is paying rent, that they can't make this directive of being neat. I'm not advocating weekly inspections, but the parent is the landlord and has the right to ask for neatness up to a point. My one friend said her son would have dirty dishes, partially eaten food under dirty clothes, and such. This isn't healthy, let alone pleasant. Keep your requirements to a minimum, however. They are learning to multi-task and prioritize. Also, if the young adult is not independent, they need to be respectful of their residency. It is about appreciation and respect as much as learning life skills.

The Extras

A Passport

Rather than send a kid to college, I would have all high school students travel. Growing up in the Midwest close to Canada, my family took a few trips along the St. Lawrence Seaway, which is the route from the Great Lakes out to the Atlantic Ocean. In Quebec, I got to hear and practice my French, and just being in a country that isn't ours is an eye opener. I had gotten passports for my sons to take them to Europe upon Adam's high school graduation and they both have used them several times since.

Adam has a friend who has a father with a condo and a large fishing boat in Cabo San Lucas, Mexico. Having gone to school in San Diego and speaking some Spanish, Adam has traveled with friends several times across the border and to Cabo San Lucas. It used to be that Americans didn't need a passport to cross the border to Canada and Mexico, but that is changing. I think also that we are going to see more travel back and forth to our neighboring countries. I have several friends entering retirement years and looking at American retirement communities in Mexico. There is an explosion of retirees there building up American communities because the weather is nice and the cost of living is so much lower. As my friend, Elizabeth, said she can rent a furnished two-bedroom home on a lake with a gardener and maid for $600 a month. As family members retire there, we might see more of us vacationing in these spots.

Similarly, I took Richard and a friend up the West Coast to Vancouver, Canada to look at colleges and universities in their junior year of high school. It was a great road trip and we met friends in Seattle who came along and it turned into a fun vacation. The cost of going to school even as an *out of state* student was cheaper there than some of the schools we were looking at here. The cost of living again was cheaper and the Canadians are such friendly people. Unless you go to Canada, there is a presumption that they speak English and are just like us. It isn't true. They have a different culture and are very proud of it. It was a delightful experience for the boys. So even if you can't imagine your young adult traveling, try it as a family adventure.

It doesn't hurt to get the passport whether or not there are travel plans. They are good for ten years. There is also a passport card and an e-passport. Things are changing in anticipation of travel and national security interests. But the process is easy. Generally, you need a passport photo that many drugstore chains will do in their photo areas, and a birth certificate. You can find sites online where you can go to apply as it has to be in person. The most common places are post offices, libraries, and City Clerk or County Clerk offices. If you don't have access to online sources, contact your local library. The good thing about a passport is that it is also a great piece of identification. If your teen doesn't have a driver's license yet, this is a good place to start to at least have an ID.

If you get a passport early, it takes the stress out of the process for when you need it. I have so many friends who have found themselves ready to go to the Caribbean or on a cruise outside of the country and at the last minute realize that they needed a passport. As with most government processes, it takes time, sometimes weeks and months, to get them unless you want to pay expensive expedited fees. A passport isn't cheap to begin with: at this printing it is $100 (and only $45 to get a passport card for only sea or land travel). Of course, since it lasts ten years the cost seems less prohibitive. We did it for Justin for an ID before he got his driver's license. Having gone to Hawaii a while back, he now wishes to save and travel to the Caribbean or Polynesia. It is hard enough for most people to make the travel plans, the plane tickets, the hotels, the show tickets and such without dealing with the passport process.

Volunteer Work

If your teen or young adult isn't working, it is a good idea for them to do some volunteer work. Most high schools encourage or even require this as it builds a resume for applying to colleges. But as we talked before, it also builds a job resume and an interest base. When Justin moved in with us, I brought him to a volunteer program I ran. It gave him a social outlet and helped develop some of his skills. He took well to leadership roles in the program and realized that is a talent he possessed and wanted to develop. It isn't unusual when your young adult has come home to live to not get a job. It is possible that they are experiencing depression, and a good way to push through that inertia is to work and have a routine. Until they get a job, they need to be doing something.

Volunteer work also gets them to focus on where their interests lie. When I hear of college students who don't know what they want to major in or when young adults aren't sure what career they want, I'm amazed. If you are paying for such an expensive education, indecision is ridiculous. Pick something. Do something. From there you can begin to narrow your interests and from there you can learn more about who you are. Indecision should be a brief moment, not an extended residence.

Volunteer work is a good place to learn to network and to develop relationships for references and possible employment down the road. The same work that went into developing oneself for college applications needs to be going into building a work resume. I always hear people talk about "looking good on a college application" but almost never hear the same said about "looking good on a job resume." Yet if the reason most parents send their young people to college is for a good job, building that resume should be going at the same time as building a college application. The eye should very much be on the job resume. The reality is that of the few going to college, fewer are graduating. The job resume will determine where they will qualify and for that they need some previous work, paid or unpaid (as in volunteer work), and references of people who have seen them work.

Chapter 10 Skills My Teen Needs to Have

As with many decisions, you should insist that they work, but let them decide where they want to volunteer. They need to be deciding who they are going to be. As well as you think you know them, they are like gift boxes ready to surprise you. My generation wasn't as big on volunteerism as is the case for schools and religious organizations today. Many high schools and even middle schools require volunteer hours. For those of you who haven't a clue where to begin, let's begin with your young adult. As with jobs, don't involve them volunteering for your business. The idea is to let them develop working skills with others and develop interest areas for possible career pathways. Don't forget it is equally valuable to find out if they are not in their field of interest. This is another opportunity to sit down and work the situation, not the kid. This meeting is time to have a dialogue. Include in the discussion how long they wish to volunteer and the number of hours per week. Six months looks good on a resume or even better is a year if they like it. It will give their reference people a chance to really get to know them.

When my sons were doing it for their high school units, it depended very much on their personality as to what they liked. My oldest son liked working outdoors and found cleanup projects of local parks and beaches matched his personality. He was always a youngster with lots of energy and needed ways to burn it off. My younger son, Richard, did some beach restoration which wasn't concerned about picking up garbage but rather pulling out non-native plants that had over run the native plants. He also did some volunteer work related to feeding the hungry. It gave him more emotional reward to do that work knowing that others benefitted from his work. I know of other young people who have volunteered in election campaigns and for the government. One mother confided to me that her son had always wanted to be a vet. However, once he did some volunteer work with animals, that went out the window. Wherever the interest is, go inquire or have your teen or young adult inquire. Research is important. They should research volunteer programs and the companies that might interest them. They can work for companies as much as volunteer for non-profit organizations. We are looking to get some idea of interests and get the recommendations and experience to decide if this is a career pathway worth pursuing.

When Richard entertained thoughts of going into modeling or ad work as a young teen, I contacted a professional actor I knew through a friend. He had lots of ideas on how to work in indy films locally or at colleges. Once you start talking to people in the field, you begin to know more about the ins and outs of that field, who is in it and where you can create a niche, first as a volunteer, later perhaps in a paid position. This also teaches the skill of how to find jobs in a field by getting into it and creating connections and working connections. Once your young adult learns how to do this sort of research and connecting, it is a skill that stays a lifetime. Sometimes it takes a while to process all the information. I myself have trouble with just the emotional time it takes to process these things, but all change needs some lag time to catch up emotionally. If momentum is going stay with it, sometimes you need to stop and take a look around at the place you have come to. This is true for your young adult and for you. However, it is important not to let a moment or day to rest and process become a time of inertia again. It is always good to set some further next steps to look to and take on after a respite.

I can't stress enough how important it is to have a game plan for all of the skill sets you are helping your young adult to develop. Volunteer work has to be a part of the big picture. You are looking to help them learn to manage work time and helping them develop work skills. This is a critical area for the job resume. Parents need to stop thinking of how this is first going to build the college application and instead make the job resume the first priority. This volunteer work will help decide their interests also. When we do this, the college piece falls into place. College isn't a career. We really need to be doing the work outside of college that guides where college is best going to suit the personality and career. Get creative about what sorts of volunteer activities are available or can be created. If a program doesn't exist in your teen or young adult's area of interest, find out how you can create one.

I've heard Cesar Millan, the Dog Whisperer, talk about how he was a dog walker and a dog groomer. It is always wise not to get too attached to what your teen or young adult wants to do. I think if Justin had a driver's license, he very well could have become a dog walker for one of the local businesses and learned the trade and gotten together his own dog walking business. But what little we did do in that way at the time taught him how to look for customers and what it took to generate interest. It got him thinking in terms of opportunity. He is very good at customer service with an eye for building the business he works in and he likes doing that. It is his interest area. It really is a mind-set to get out and start creating what you want and exploring what you want. In every young person I see who has developed this sense of exploration and moving his or her career forward, it becomes a way of approaching many facets of life. Start with the interest and then connect to people who are in it and ask for leads. Having grown up with Drill Sergeant type parents, I was always afraid to ask for help or *bother* people. The funny thing is that most people enjoy sharing what they know and being treated like an expert. It lets them be creative without taking the risks of searching things out and they get credit for the idea. When I run volunteer projects, I am always asking for input. People enjoy participating in designing a better system or making something run smoother. Not all connections or ideas will pan out, but in a way you are becoming an expert and gaining valuable knowledge of the career you want and don't want. Whether it works or doesn't work, you are learning and that is what you want to instill.

Let me tell you one quick thing I've learned from picking people's brains. A person can seem very knowledgeable about something but sometimes you need to learn to talk to more than one person. We all have a habit of wanting to find that one person we can rely on. For example, many of us have a favorite mechanic we trust absolutely. In my parents' generation, there was a tendency to frequent the same doctor, the same stores, the same dentist, and the same grocer. Professionals and businesses sought and maintained a loyalty and a bond with customers. With workers being more temporary and moving and relocating, both businesses and employees are less concerned with that loyalty base today. My parents would never change a doctor, yet today you get assigned different doctors in your health plan or at clinics, and the importance of a bond is fairly low. We are consumers and will go where we get the best service or deal. I have found that we have to learn to be good researchers and interviewers. We need to teach our young adults to find people we are comfortable with and who match our personalities. These make for good work skills as, sooner or later, you have to interview people for positions and conversely, you will be interviewed. A good job candidate learns to be an interviewer themselves. They have to make a decision about a job and job pay. They have to evaluate other workers on their team. These are valuable skills that are never addressed in traditional school curriculum.

Volunteer work and paid work bring confidence. Work and responsibility are hallmarks of adulthood. Studying is a great skill for college and school but it is work that is the focus of adulthood and the ultimate goal for most parents sending their kids off to college. Studying alone at the expense of the work record paid or otherwise is a foolish bargain. I've seen some brilliant students who are clueless about navigating a career and a good job. In this skill set of work and work ethics, you can be an enormous help directing and supporting your young adult.

Investment education

So far, Richard's goals after graduating from college are in investing. There was a period in his high school days when all the boys were playing poker and it was all the rage. I know Richard's grandfather liked to go to Reno or Las Vegas and I worried there might be a gambling gene on the loose. I remember one New Year's, Richard's grandfather and grandmother were being flown to Reno with other people with a gambling bent to a casino where they would also be given a room to ring in the New Year. I knew then that most likely grandfather had probably played more than the slot machines. I knew they went to one of the gambling Meccas a few times a year. I could be wrong, but I didn't know anyone else getting such a nice deal. I decided that if Richard had that gene, I would at least try to channel it. I offered to set up an Ameritrade account for him and we would learn about investment. His uncle, John had gotten pretty good at it and gave us advice. We subscribed to the *Investor Business Daily* which I had become acquainted with at Tony Robbins' Wealth Mastery seminar.

The seminar had been held in scenic Aspen, Colorado one lovely spring week. We heard various speakers talk about different approaches to investing and learned about finances and how to manage them. We had homework assignments to get to know the layout of *Investment Business Daily* and how to read stock charts. It was intense for a girl like me, coming from a working class background and always living in fear of not enough money. For the first time in my life I felt empowered to utilize money and not be a slave to it. Although my sons' father was a doctor, he too had grown up with a father who handled all of his life's decisions including money. I didn't want my sons to have that attitude that they should be afraid of money, where to get it, how to have enough and stay safe because those were the concerns of my family and most families I knew. At long last, at this seminar I began to see money in a different light.

When I came home from that seminar, I told Richard it was time he and I learned about investing. He was about 14 and he looked at me like a deer in the headlights. He just sort of said, "Me?" I said, "I've seen on talk shows experiments where they have a monkey throw a dart at a board of investments and invest in what he hit and then follow what experts recommended. Oddly enough, the random hits of the monkey did better. So we can give it a shot." Uncle John said he'd help and off we went on our great adventure. It is easy to set up an account online. You can call and get a bit of help, and of course there are all sorts of online classes, investments seminars in your community, books on investment, and the like. You can find a mentor like we found in Uncle John. Get the *Investor's Business Daily* as it is much more current than monthly or weekly investment magazines. If you don't want to pay the subscription fee, go to the library. Research and learning are a great way to start this sort of adventure. You can start small while you are learning. Uncle John confessed he made a few hefty mistakes in his first year of learning but later on made enough in a few months to buy his daughter a car.

I'm not advocating day trading or any style or system, but I think the idea that your money should make money is important and if the gambling gene runs in your veins, this is a way to learn and earn. As with all else, these are approaches to obtaining skills that bode well for many aspects of living. The sad part of life is that we all will be taken advantage of and we all will take some risks and lose. It is just the way of life. But to be able to get up, learn, and move on is critical for survival in the same way surviving disease and injury was for our ancestors. Avoidance of life's ills is one way to survive, but learning how to spring back, to roll with the punches, is another. You need both. A single survival tactic isn't enough. Managing money and learning how money works is an important survival skill in the ever-changing world economy and national economy.

Richard and I hit a busy year and didn't have much chance to manage our investment accounts. It sat quietly and actually made money. That was good to know also. In all of this, we are learning. Knowledge is power. On his college applications, Richard spoke with confidence about investing. I felt more confident about at least navigating the systems of investing. In the end, we gained some good memories of doing this together. In addition to attaining skills for your young adult and even for yourself because we continue to grow through all our life phases, learning this skill also increases the building of memories. This is a great way to share strategies and ideas about where to go and where businesses are going. It gives you a place to start talking to each other about a topic. This is a good thing in developing adult-to-adult relationships.

Vacations and Time Together

I remember talking to my youngest sister once about some pleasant childhood memories. There had been so much yelling and criticism growing up that, for the longest time, I thought I didn't have any good childhood memories. After taking the Tony Robbins course and realizing life is what you focus on, I began to go back and look for some of the good memories, even if I thought they would be very few. I had to look first at little things like warm spring days, colored holiday lights in the snowy winter evenings, and such, but then I got so I could pull up a few pleasant memories with my parents. This is why I try to get parents to put more positive interactions in force during each day with their teens and young adults rather than the negative nagging, talking down to them days that are so common in family life. My sister was the youngest and was only ten years old when I left home at age 18 for college and the work world. Her memories of me were vague and my experience of the family was different being the oldest. We were crowded and poorer until my mother had more time to sell Avon beauty products and supplement my father's factory work income. When the family was young, it was hard to carve out that sort of time, but as I got older around 11 or 12 and could babysit toddlers, she began going out to sell more during the day.

My mother had regular customers that she would often give the orders to with the promise to pay come pay day. Being a homemaker back in the day when mothers

Chapter 10 Skills My Teen Needs to Have

seldom did volunteer work in the schools and communities, selling was also her social life. She got to know mothers in other neighborhoods and know their relatives and friends as she was referred to them. She got to hear all the juicy gossip and let's be honest probably passed some on. Sometimes she would take me along and send me up to the door to collect on payday when she was running short on time or was irritated with a customer who hadn't paid in a timely manner. These were kind of special times. It was just the two of us and the big treat would be to swing by Burger King. For a working class family, eating out was going to McDonald's or A&W Hot Dogs. We never even had pizza ordered out, a food I discovered as a college student. For once my mother was chatting with me, having pleasant talks. I loved those times. My sister recounted the same thing was part of her childhood. For both of us, those had been nice memories, real mother daughter times. It doesn't take much.

When my children were young, I loved having family vacations to Disneyland and, as they got older, winter skiing trips. I became a co-den mother for Richard's Cub Scout den and then added to these were the summer camping trips with scouts and with another family we skied with in the winter. My own parents would take a yearly trip with us in a fold out camper. We went to lakes and parks but also up through Canada and over to Washington, D.C. and to the east coast. The camper gave us a place to stay and a place to cook cheap and filling meals. While there was some yelling as you might expect with six kids, there were a number of nice memories, too. It was that togetherness I wanted to recreate. Even now, I try to take my sons on trips. I said to my friend, Anne, in Switzerland when we stayed with her and her family that I wanted these times before they went off on their own and no longer cared to travel with good ol' mom. Anne laughed and said they will still go when they leave home if it is some place that interests them! So these days I try to find fun places to go as a family and was rewarded not too long ago when Adam checked in with me to see if I had any summer trips planned for us. Considering he is partially in the work world while finishing his studies, I was flattered. Time off is becoming more precious to him as an adult.

I know of too many parents who, if they do make time to go away, don't make it to somewhere fun for their teen or young adult. I suspect this is because it hasn't been something they've done often and are at a bit of a loss about what to do to make these trips or time together a success. When I took my sons to Washington, D.C. in their teens, I planned out our sights and interests as I always had. I was a bit surprised to suddenly start getting questions and requests for sights they were interested in. I went along with the choices as best I could and loved it. Even in Europe, we improvised some activities based on what they wanted to see. We stumbled one day on a racecar performance in downtown London. They had cleared a section of streets and raced these individual high performance racecars down them doing *doughnuts* and other stunts I knew nothing about. My sons wanted to watch despite the crowds, the fact that cars zoomed by at long intervals, and the noise reverberating off the downtown buildings was deafening. But this was an experience and why not let them have this part of the trip? Be someone fun to travel with and have a good time. We all know family members or even friends who bring their complaints and negative comments to experiences and adventures. They color everything in black or brown. I love when Dr. Phil asks a particularly negative and complaining family member, "How much fun are you to live with?" They always look shocked as if it had never occurred to them that maybe they are a source of unpleasantness.

If you think that is just not very important, I point again to the fact that in these circumstances, you are keenly under the model microscope. Your teen or young adult sees how you handle new situations, dealing with vendors in strange places, transportation, navigating the area, and the routine. When I taught Justin to drive, one thing I told him was that if you miss a turn off, just keep going and find a place to turn around. It was my pet peeve to watch dangerous drivers go careening over several lanes to wildly make a last minute exit or turn. One exercise I had him do once was to pretend that he had missed the last exit to the San Mateo Bridge. This is a bridge down the peninsula from San Francisco that crosses the San Francisco Bay and is about seven miles long. I said, "Things happen and if you make a mistake don't panic, just deal with it."

I love to rent cars when I travel and find my way around new places. I routinely get lost but find out some new places to see or make note of grocery stores or drug stores and the like should I need them. Justin and I have traveled to Hawaii and Las Vegas and he gets to see me in action getting lost. We just make note of places while I find my way back. Sometimes I even find better routes for getting around. I don't waste my learning experience.

I was a bit surprised when he told me one day early in his driving career that he was running an errand up to San Francisco and got lost. He recounted the story and said he wished he could remember exactly where he had been getting back on path because he had seen an interesting restaurant he might want to visit in the future. It was then that I realized that he was modeling my behavior. I myself had improved upon my parents' behavior in navigating new places. My mother loved the sense of adventure and was of course the navigator while my father drove. Too often in reading the map and trying to get oriented she spoke up too late about a turn that should have been made. My dad would get flustered as most people would and she would try to find a different route to achieve our end destination. I remember her trying to be calm and even joking about it and I realize that is what I do and have passed the behavior along to all my children. In the end, we can model problem solving instead of emotional reactions that trigger more emotional reactions in others and leave a bad memory.

I have had great vacations with my children. It is the quality time that we need to bond as a family, especially as they have their studies, jobs, and routines. *Quality time* used to be the mantra for divorced families sharing custody. Maybe one parent didn't have the most physical custody, but the time they did have the children became *quality time* and that was the focus and end goal for having some time together. Perhaps in this day and age we need to refocus our priorities in that direction for families in general. Is this going to launch your young adult? Not directly, but it does by creating a bond where they will model on your success and will handle life with more confidence. If we can model well and set appropriate skill challenges for independence then we have truly done our job right for that stage of life. ✑

Chapter 11 Rut Thinkers and the College Fairy

I have a lovely little white dog that is a terrier and poodle mix. She is almost 15 years old and we rescued Princess from the S.P.C.A when she was barely one year-old. She has ruled the house ever since. Princess and I take two walks a day. We take a short one in the morning and a long one at night. When it is the weekend or a holiday, her favorite place to walk is a block away, on the large elementary school grounds where my sons had gone long ago. I think Princess likes all the kid smells of lunches dropped and since the school has a huge field on a bluff with a view to San Francisco some 20 miles away, I am happy, too. I used to notice when my sons were at soccer practice or baseball practices in the late fall or early spring and as the sun went down, little white tail rabbits with brownish fur ran along the fence line. In the late afternoon they probably hoped they could blend in with the ground better than when the sun was more overhead, highlighting their movements. In our area, we have beautiful but deadly predator birds. I've seen the golden eagles and hawks looking for tasty rabbits along with the pigeons I feed in my backyard, and sometimes they succeed in their dramatic quests. One day my poor housekeeper was doing dishes in the kitchen and I was chatting and paying bills when this bullet like thing hit one of the pigeons and feathers scattered all over the yard and into the pool. This majestic golden eagle, I believe, stood on the dazed or dead bird, daring anyone to come near. We were dumbstruck how fast it happened. When survival is that basic, it can seem very brutal. Most of us have the fear that pigeon must have lived with until the end, that something out there will get you.

I noticed in my walk with Princess that over the years the rabbits have worn the grass in these paths and created ruts, or places so worn down there is little grass or greenery. A lush and beautiful field with a few trees lies open to them but their lives are lived pretty much along these ruts. I began to picture some of the people I talk to who can't seem to open their minds to new ideas or more than one option as these rabbits running in their same old ruts. For me, they live as rut thinkers though quite often are very highly educated people. Like these lovely little rabbits, they will forsake greener pastures to stay in their ruts.

My generation, the Baby Boomers have become incredible rut thinkers when it comes to the concept of college as the end all and be all to a successful career and job security. Even in the face of emerging statistics that half of all college kids graduating will go home to live with Mom and Dad, we repeat the same mantras and refuse to reassess what is going wrong with the system. We pressure our kids and we pressure ourselves to make our kids go to college. It is the only answer. Our so-called *career centers* in schools are really college centers first and foremost. Standardized testing that ruins self-esteem and real education of our young is a billion dollar industry and has no desire for us to re-evaluate the folly of this mindset. How can we call ourselves educated when we can't even look at reality but instead prefer old thinking, old ruts?

If you imagine that you view life like that field and you have to cross it to get to better safety or better food, will you make rabbit ruts? Most of us will. Some people call it a game plan but as the game progresses don't you make new plans to accommodate new information? For rut thinkers, all they can see is the one rut out in front of them and they are running down it as fast as they can in hopes that something won't get them. On occasion they will jump into their neighbor's rut and run for a while. But that is the best they can do for adjusting game plans. And historically it made sense. After all, death was a much more pressing reality. Without vaccinations, medicines, or treatments, your life expectancy wasn't so great. The best you could hope for was some way to make a living and raise your family. You worked on the farm until you couldn't anymore or you worked in the factory until you retired. This was the same with other professions. You worked until you were worn out. The rut was stable and comfortable because there were plenty of other things in life that shook up that safety and security. Illness, death, plagues, natural disasters such as tornados, floods, earthquakes, fires and wars all loomed like the eagles or hawks hovering over the field.

Where I grew up in Michigan, the town was peppered with car factories. The ideal life was to go to work in a factory, get good benefits, have a good retirement package, and retire in 30-40 years. My dad did this. A lot of my schoolmates and their parents did this. But at the last high school reunion I attended, I was struck by how lost people were. The car factories were moving to the South, where labor and resources were cheap. Many people took early retirement, and now in their 50's with smaller families who had grown up, they were lost as to how they might live out these golden years of early retirement. It was that deer in the headlights look. At their age, people are having vibrant careers as leaders, senators, judges, Supreme Court justices, and CEO's. The experience of age and good health have made others valuable commodities and at the top of their game. But for this group, the rut is over. If they have defined themselves as their rut, then who are they? When I have suggested to learn something new, start a new career, the one they always wanted, their reply is "I'm too old" or "I could never do that." Why not? Because they believe they are the rut. And as we are models for our children who may be young adults, what are we telling them? That they should be the rut?

Using Jim Fay's characterization of parent types, the Helicopter parent, the Drill Sergeant parent, and the Consultant parents, most of us were raised by one of the first two or a combination of the first two. Our goal for a healthy teens and young adults is to be like the third type, the Consultant, or as I prefer to call them, the Coach parents. The reality is that we tend to be like our parents, either the Helicopter or the Drill Sergeant or both. Rut thinkers are prone to using the Helicopter style or the Drill Sergeant style. I'm not sure what comes first, the parenting style or the rut thinking looking for a parent style that has a rut to it. It's sort of like asking which came first, the chicken or the egg? I think the rut came first just as I think the egg came first, but that's another book. If you stop being the rut, you flow into being the Counselor parent. You are looking out over the field now for the best place for you to go. You choose. And then you can respect that others need to choose and that not all paths work for all people. What factors you use to cross the field may not be the same factors others would choose and there is nothing wrong with that.

Chapter 11 Rut Thinkers and the College Fairy

So let's talk about the very hidden but the biggest driving force of parents of teens and young adults which is the College Fairy. The path to the College Fairy has a great connection to rabbit rut thinkers and to the Helicopter and Drill Sergeant parenting styles. As the rabbit rut thinker, long ago you were told that people who go to college make more money that those who don't. This is called a *correlation*. A *correlation* means that there is a connection. Either it is a cause and effect connection or there is some other factor or factors present that link the two. For example, let's say that all kids who drink milk graduate from kindergarten. Does that mean if you took a child and made sure they drank milk that they would graduate from kindergarten even if they didn't attend? No. You think that is silly but if there is a complex situation, sometimes you can't see all the factors creating the outcome. Maybe you only see the two and it is easy to assume they are cause and effect. We assumed about 40 years ago, when college was pretty much for the wealthy, that there was a cause and effect. You were wealthy or stayed wealthy in part because you went to college. Little did we know that maybe these people would have made more money anyway because they came from money! They had connections to people with money, they had opportunities available to them because they had money to invest, and being with other moneyed people in college, they married money. So yes, if you went to college then, more likely than not you made more money than people who didn't, but it may have been other factors that were in play and not just that correlation.

Things changed with WWII when the G.I. bill paid for college. Now people could go to college with wealthier people and they could get into the moneyed loop. With degrees not being so common, it did tend to open doors and opportunities even if you didn't marry money or utilize your new connections. For my generation, the Viet Nam war drove many young men into college as a way to avoid the draft. For a long time, college attendance took young men out of the draft, but eventually a lottery was developed to send even college men to Viet Nam unless they were in certain excluded categories such as medical school. Where young men went, young women followed. Many women went to college to marry a college guy, since before the birth control pill a woman still planned to stay home and raise a family as her primary career in life. I remember one dorm mate who loved to brag that she had the dress, the ceremony planned, the day picked out, and all she needed was to find the man! That was not uncommon.

So the correlation became gospel. If you go to college, you will get a good job. I hear it all the time today. No one stops to question it; it is assumed as the rut to jump into. After all, many of us from the working class and middle class didn't have these opportunities before to create new and bigger dreams, to network and figure out how to get there with our degree or degrees in hand. As you can see, perhaps it was the opportunities to dream that were as powerful as the degree, but there were no studies on that. However, some new studies are showing that if you make the dreams and the plans, you are more likely to achieve to them. Tony Robbins discusses this in one of his motivational tapes. He explains that a group from an Ivy League school was tracked over about 20 years. Those that had concrete goals and plans when they graduated were much more likely to be on target and wealthy than their fellow graduates some 20 years later. Setting dreams and making plans to get to those dreams is the real path, not the degree.

Most of us baby boomers have followed that mantra that says to get our college degrees and then we will make more money, and we have sent our children on this quest. As colleges were once the provinces of the rich, a certain snobbery has percolated down to the classes in getting a degree. There is still a tendency to put others down for not going on to college. It is as if they were too dumb to go to college, yet our own college bound darlings are, by virtue of following the college degree rut, the only ones to find high paying jobs. The snobbery is alive and well in all the classes of society. When students and their parents talk about going to a *good school*, what do they mean? Early in our country's history it was the Ivy League schools, the prestigious schools with reputations of being where the best of the wealthy went. A good school in short had prestigious students and their families. This was the opportunity to make connections with those who are in power by virtue of wealth and connections, not necessarily because of becoming more educated at that school than at other schools. It is about who is in those schools and the wealth and power of those families. Even for the wealthy, it is as much the job of a student to be making connections for opportunities as it is to study. Frequently, wealthy people will talk about the quality of wealth and social status their young adults are being exposed to. I seldom hear that emphasis in middle and lower income parents and students. A good school is still thought to be a path of the best education and thus the best candidate for a job. These parents instead believe in the College Fairy.

Every talk I give, I know I am talking to believers in the College Fairy who is as real to them as Santa was to me as a child. When I was about five years old, I was in bed upstairs in our duplex, not getting to sleep very well. I was waiting to hear Santa arriving and was just beyond myself with excitement. Toys. Lots and lots of toys, I silently prayed. I then heard a knock on the door downstairs and my mother answered the door and joyously shouted, "Santa!" Hey, we didn't have a fireplace; Santa could knock at the door! I heard him say, "Ho, ho, merry Christmas!" and in he came and I heard nothing else, relieved that he had arrived. I believed in Santa until I was eight years old. At that time, I noticed that my mother's distinctive handwriting and Santa's writing on gifts was very much alike. It didn't help that kids in the third grade were divided over the issue of whether or not there was a Santa. I knew for sure because I had heard him. I had proof! So when I casually asked my mother why her and Santa's handwriting was the same, she took me out of ear shot of my siblings and told me the truth. I had not wanted to hear that! I wanted to hear that she and Santa had learned from the same book, anything but that she was Santa. I told her that couldn't be and how I heard Santa when I was five years-old and we were living in the other house. She thought for a minute and then laughed. Uncle Kenny had popped by with some gifts from grandma. They were just joking around. Isn't it funny how we draw wrong conclusions from correlations? I'm still not happy about that Santa thing but maybe that is why I learned to be more careful about assuming causation for every connection found. We all get a little sloppy in our thinking.

So now as I give my talks I know that the little five year-old kids in some people are screaming in their minds that I am wrong. That you go to a good pre-school, you get into a good elementary school, then a good middle school, then a good high school, take some tests, score really high, take advanced standing classes where you have to become a scholarly hermit, get into a good college, and there she is waiting for you at the end of the line-the College Fairy! "Give me your degree and I will give you your six figure job and you will live happily ever after in the job of your dreams," she says while

Chapter 11 Rut Thinkers and the College Fairy

your parents look on, beaming with pride. What I see in reality are stunned parents as their adult kids move back home, with no job and no idea of what they want and no College Fairy whatsoever. This can't be! Stubbornly, some people send their kids back for the advanced degree, ever hopeful that their child missed the College Fairy visit but will absolutely be there when they get that Master's or PhD. Why? It is because some people do seem to succeed at this scenario. They seem to glide along in the rut, or rather the college track laid out long ago, and have the great job and great career with little fuss or muss. Ah, but was that all they were doing, the academics, to be the best and score the best, or were they also networking, interning, working in their field and had figured out who they were along the way and had support for that? Often we mistakenly assume it all came from college.

I knew I was making headway when my friend Ruth came to me with a story. I repeatedly tell parents, even friends, that the key is finding out what your child wants to do and get them into the field to see if that is true and support whatever path they take. Ruth, like so many others, was doing the College Fairy mantra and wanted to get her only son, Donald, to go through college. As he was approaching his senior year in high school, she was despairing. Donald had never been great with classes and homework but he did fairly well. He was fabulous in sports. He lived, ate, and breathed some sport all year round. In some he was a star, in others a solid and good player. For a divorced, single mom this was a great way for her son to be around adult male role models. He worked well in the park and recreation departments with children and considered maybe he'd be a high school coach one day. But as classes became more difficult and her own financial situation more tenuous, she wasn't so sure that this was at all workable. She endured months of me saying that we have to get away from this model of everyone going to college. There are degrees you can get online, there are vocational schools where you can get your AA (the two year associate's degree) in 18 months with a skill and job placement, and there are so many other options than just get that degree.

Like so many, she would agree and then the mantra of going to college would begin again. The pressures come from all of our peers and the schools. Stay in the rut, be the rut, run the rut, and above all believe in the College Fairy or maybe you aren't such a good parent, right? Then one day, Ruth was telling me how she was talking to another mom whose son was on the same team as Donald. The mother asked where Donald wanted to go to college and for the first time I ever heard, she said she wasn't sure where Donald was going or if he needed to go. She confided that they needed to look at some options and Donald had to figure out what he wanted. The other mom was shocked and praised Ruth for being so open and supportive and seemed inspired to rethink her own son's future. Ruth had become a role model for escaping the rut. And Ruth looked more confident and less worried than I had seen her around the topic in years. When you leave the rut, you can focus on your relationship with your almost adult child, you can reconnect. You become a human again, a loving parent, and not a rabbit rut thinker.

Ruth isn't the only one. I love to watch the light bulb go on with people when they poke their heads out of the rut. There's a whole field out there! Lots of choices and you can tailor them to your needs and not run the rut. People also get mad. Why have our schools turned their backs on the two thirds of students for whom college is not the way, at least not in the immediate future? We are consumers of education but we behave as if we are lucky to be allowed into the education system and we take everything dished out to us if we are allowed to stay. We need to start acting like the consumers we are. I am dumbfounded by the new way to get parents to pay for more years in college. That method is the *impacted major*, meaning that there are more students needing a class than there are teachers for them. Most majors have two years of fairly mindless and irrelevant general education classes. By requiring students to keep trying to get them all in along with the classes to fulfill their majors, students are frequently going in the summers or an extra fifth year. Instead of complaining, parents gladly pay the extra year of tuition. It doesn't occur to them that if the college made the requirement and the student had trouble getting the class because of over-enrollment, then they could also waive the requirement or find a substitute so that the student could finish in four years. We don't need to follow the ruts. Success is not in the ruts. ✍

Chapter 12 If Not College, Then What?

The two biggest problems that at-home, dependent young adults face are finding a livelihood and acquiring skills sets that create independence. We assume that our education system is handling both when they are handling neither. The reality of that comes home very quickly when the adult child either fails to leave home after high school or returns home after some stint in college. In this chapter we will look at finding out ways to get your child gainfully employed and get you to develop a game plan toward a good job or career with or without college.

However, I have a quick note for those whose children do seem bent on the college track in high school. I was one of those kids and my youngest son was, too. I watch these high school years with dread. We parents are so uneducated on the best way to get into college. We assume it is as it was for us; good grades, good extra-curricular activities, and good test scores. There is a better way to do it. Your student should start taking courses at the community college. In most states, maybe all, you can take community college courses in high school. In California, you won't be charged tuition. You could take two years and obtain your Associate's Degree while in high school so long as you get your high school diploma or GED before applying for your Associates Degree. This will not only knock out a number of the boring general ed classes taught in the four year colleges, but at the community college level you will be taught by professors and not by teaching assistants for the most part. It also changes how colleges look at you. You are no longer *just* a high school student but a college student looking to come in, and that looks much better than the old way we did it. The colleges are now seeing your grades in college and the fact that you are ambitious enough to do this. The reason for all the testing and hoops that colleges put high school students through is that they are looking for predictors of probable college success. Once they choose your child for their school they are hoping that they will have you and your money for the next five years, four years if you are lucky. Remember half of all students entering college won't graduate from a four year program. That's a lot of lost revenue. I am absolutely positive that my oldest son was accepted into all but one of the colleges he applied to because he had two community college classes under his belt for which he got "A's". He also had the recommendation of those professors. I tell parents of exceptionally bright students not to waste time on those high school honor classes and advanced classes. If your student is that bright, they should be in college classes. They are much more stimulating than high school and what a great deal on tuition for you! Had I known, I would have put my sons in more community college classes because high school classes bored them to tears at times. We might have saved a year's worth of tuition between them had they taken those classes. If your child is that bright, send them to the next level. Don't waste time in high school. It is going to look light years ahead of their peers if you do that and this is a great way to start looking at college majors and maybe trying a few out. It is a winning situation across the board. They save money for you, get challenged, and are much more likely to get into the college of their dreams. For those colleges, they are looking like a sure bet, and colleges do care about their bottom line.

The College Track Toward Employment

We need to put into perspective how college correlates to a *good job*. The goal of colleges has never been to provide you a base of employment. As recently as 2005, when I was taking a biology class at a local community college so that I could qualify to take the patent exam, I heard a young woman say that, "the goal of college was to make her a well rounded person." Her major was French literature. I don't know about you, but all the job ads I've looked at have never asked for a "well rounded person" for their job position. I haven't even seen a job ad for a professional student although I could sure qualify in that, with all my career changes! Yet we assume that by sending our children down the college path, they will arrive at a job. But where is the preparation for that? If there is one big culprit here it is that no one is teaching the soft skills to land a job and we aren't requiring our teens and young adults to get job training to prepare for the work world. Parents aren't doing it and neither are high schools or colleges for the most part. Because it takes forever for change to happen in education, we parents need to reinstitute the work ethic and experience in our young.

What do jobs want? I sit on the steering committee for our high school Career Tech program. The Career Tech program grew out of the Academy tradition that began during the late 1960s and 1970s. When I was in high school, we were tracked depending on where we wanted to go after high school. There was the college track, the business track for males and females wanting to be secretaries and business people, and there was the job skills track like automotive and other skilled employment. Tracks were eliminated as it became apparent that the Caucasians were in the college track and the other ethnic minorities were put into work track or business track. The idea was to make college access available to everyone but very quickly it became evident that not everyone cared for the highly academic program of one size fits all. This was the time of the birth of the academy. Academies were "schools within a school" and dealt with the problem of "at risk students" who were doing poorly in school and might drop out, or worse, get kicked out of school. Academies formed to help these students get on track. They were given mentors, job internships, and academic help to stay involved and engaged in school. College is an option as many do make honor rolls with this kind of support, but a focus toward a well paying career is the real drive in these programs. Today, with business leaders involved, they are also getting access to teens as they are trained and can offer these students jobs at the end of high school or the end of college. Quite frankly, this should be the focus of most of school. "Academics only" as the only way to success is a dismal failure. A good job is obtained not just by academics but along with a good work resume and work experience.

At one of our Career Tech meetings, a business leader in the construction field stated that they want experience relevant to the job and some good recommendations from people in the field. While many colleges and universities are now requiring internships, which may pay but more likely don't, as part of a degree, some degree majors don't. This immediately puts the student without experience at a huge disadvantage. They are seen as purely academic sorts with not much of anything to recommend them to

Chapter 12 If Not College, Then What?

an employer. If you are in a major such as engineering, nursing, and teaching, frequently you will be working somewhere in that field as a summer job or as part of the program to get the degree. This is great. Even in law school, the most successful job candidates had interned somewhere and got their break that way. Without interning or working in the field, your job chances go downhill. More than anything, it is experience and networking that are keys to getting a job, not a college degree. A college degree may help you advance, may help you demand more pay, but get a job? No. Parents, you have to get that and get that now. Unfortunately, parents don't get it until their graduating student comes home to live without any good job prospects. Worse, these students never looked into what the pay was within that job field or what the job really entailed. You have to be in the field to see if it is a match for you. One friend recounted to me how her 17-year-old loved to paint and thought of getting into car design. As he researched the field, he found out that the pay wasn't very good and you had to travel a lot. Neither of these would be something he would want. Had he gone blindly on through high school and college with such a dream but he would have been shocked by the realities. Not to mention that his parents would have just paid for a college degree that wasn't going to be used in that field. This is why an exploration of the field and experience in the field are crucial. We all know people who graduated in one field and were never employed in it as they floundered to find where they really belonged job wise. That is why it is important to get your teen and young adult familiar with the information interview.

In the Career Tech program of our school district, a career fair is put on every spring. This is something that schools would do well to expose all of their students to and require it. There are booths where students can go and talk to people in the field about job prospects. This helps them to learn to develop confidence in asking questions. Then a number of us are interviewers and we get to spend 15 minutes or so with a student who is dressed for an interview and brings his/her resume. Our job is to find out what job they are interviewing for and assume the role of a prospective employer. They don't know us and we don't know them so it is like a going in cold to talk to someone you don't know. They will get to go to a number of interviewers to get a feel for how to make it happen. We give feedback that is constructive and positive. We compliment what they did well and encourage improvement in other areas. I had one young man look very casually dressed for a position I knew would require a bit more formal dress. So told him he looked great for business casual but for a first interview in that field, a shirt and tie would do wonders. Young people don't have a lot of experience with these things and we were encouraging them in what is usually a very tense situation. They all gave feedback on us and could write notes to thank us. The general consensus was that the job interviews were their favorite part. Where else do you hear the good things that you are doing? We also could give them ideas for making real life connections in these fields. We were mentoring them through a difficult process that most young people do not get taught.

Encourage your teen or young adult to go to an information interview. This was something I didn't remember from my young adult days but it is very common today. It is a chance to get familiar with a field and network with people in it. It is a chance to take your resume to a professional who understands what to look for and to go through an interview process without the pressure of a job being on the line. Your teen or young adult can do what my Career Tech students did and ask for feedback. For instance, once the professional has read the resume, they can ask if the format is a good one for that field. Basically, they will ask if there is any way that it could be improved. This is best to do at the end of the interview when the interviewer has had a chance to get to know the individual and what might be important additions or deletions to the resume. There is also the opportunity to ask what sorts of opportunities and promotions to expect in the field and how to be better trained or prepared for the job. It doesn't hurt to ask about possible internships or starting jobs for gaining experience. A few of these done throughout the year will help the teen and young adult decide if the field is worth pursuing and this is the start of networking. If you are unfamiliar with informational interviews, basically, you contact someone in the business or field and request an informational interview. Most people in jobs and careers are more than happy to lend a helping hand to a newcomer as we all remember so well how awful it was for us first starting out. If you have contacted one person and they are too busy, ask if they know of someone who might be willing to give such an interview. If the company has a human resources department, you can ask them if there is a person who would be willing to do this. If you are a parent with a young adult at home, this is another way to break the logjam. Require them to go out and start doing these interviews. It may be easier for them to do an information interview than the frightening job interview. This is the way to get to know people in the field and start networking. You want a foot in the door and this says that you have initiative. It is good practice. But back to plotting a career pathway.

There are many paths through college to gainful employment. I want you out of the rut right now that says you just go to high school and college. It is not about finishing high school and going to a four-year college or a two-year college to transfer to a four-year college alone. If you are doing this, then start your research for finding the College Fairy. We parents have gotten to be a bit lazy. We aren't conversing with our young adults to find out about them and what they want and helping them. Our job is to help them plot their career pathways and progress down them. If you have a teen ready to go to college you need to help them figure out what their major is going to be. If they don't know, you really need to get to work. What are their strengths, what are their interests? Sit down and make a list with them. Take them to lunch to do this and do it a couple of times. Have them write what they think their interests are and what they think their strengths are. You write them down, also. This is all part of creating dreams that will pull them along. If there are weaknesses, don't let those stop them or you! Those are going to be challenges that will make them stronger. Research the field and look seriously at the starting pay and requirements for advancement. There has to be a game plan. Just as with a football game or other team sport, the game plan will change as the game moves forward.

Justin has an awful time with spelling. It is a major weakness for him, especially since he wants to advance in management where paperwork is a must. He used to hide this flaw but you certainly can't hide it forever. In hiding it you either look like you are in denial or not being honest. We had to come up with a way to deal with this problem area. With practice in writing for MySpace.com, doing e-mails, and text messaging, he is getting better with phonetically spelling his words. He may always have trouble but for once writing is something that is relevant to him and the motivation to communicate with peers is much more of a reward than getting good grades on boring assignments. He used to avoid talking about his difficulty writing as it was a source of shame. Too many years in special education and being made fun of made him want to pretend it didn't exist. I became his resume editor and writer but we did it together.

Chapter 12 If Not College, Then What?

We have talked about how he can handle this in job interviews and he is interested now in finding co-workers who can write or edit for him and he is comfortable with that. He is a talented people person who excels in management and marketing. As long as he addresses his weakness while building on his strengths, he can have a good career. He may always need a friend to help at work but there is nothing wrong with that. Young adults are still learning to write well as a communication; it is a skill in progress. My oldest son, Adam, has e-mailed me his college papers to edit and correct for him several times. There is nothing wrong with this. This is a way to face challenges and deal with them constructively. Too often we get critical about why they can't be perfect in assignments and skills. It is because they are learning. Remember that their brains are still in transition. I've watched Adam improve dramatically in his writing, much as Justin has. Had Justin only gone to college, he would not have done well. In the work world he is excelling and he will fit in college as he needs it. This is a much better model than blindly going to college.

So brainstorm and keep talking about how choices are working out. We adults tend to want a smooth road, pick a career or major and stay there but this is frequently not workable. This process very much depends on trial and error. It needs a lot fine-tuning along the way. Even if you find an area of interest sometimes you will find other positions or jobs better suited that are tangential to the one you started with and a better fit for your strengths and weaknesses. You want a free flow of ideas. It is like buying clothes. You can't know until you try them on if they will or won't work for you. Try on a lot of things and look for more. Any student has some idea of what classes they like, whether they feel they can be in sales, in management, or in something artistically creative. It is important to start to figure out the personality. Quite frankly, we all have a lot of talents. This will get your young adult into the frame of mind to start looking at who they are and give them a built in flexibility and resilience to situations. For example, Justin knows he can do retail work, but he can also be a personal assistant, or an animal technician, or work in the travel industry. My son Adam has numerous interests such as in sales or for jobs in the clothing industry, as he likes the business side. Yet he also likes flying planes (he has had lessons and loves it), and he loves political campaign work. Any of these areas are worth exploring to find out what might appeal at the highest level both in terms of financial success and interests. No one wants a job or career that doesn't have a chance for pay and experience advancement. My youngest son, Richard, loves investment, auctions and entrepreneur work, creating music, and is interested in non-profit work. If any one of these job careers don't pan out, all of my young adults have other industries they can turn to that they are interested in to explore new career options. It is also a good idea to turn one of the interests into a hobby. Justin can volunteer to work at the local animal shelter. Adam can volunteer in a political campaign. Richard could assist with auctions. These build up experience and give some hands on experience. We want our young adults to be able to have numerous paths and options in a shifting economy. I too have had visions of great success and a smooth road down one of the many career paths but have had to stop myself. It is a propensity of parenting in this life phase to wish to be done and back on focus in our own lives, but this is still part of the job. Our teens and young adults are explorers of life right now. That is what will give them the stories at the end of their lives to tell their grandchildren, just as we have our stories of youth and career changes and advancement. It is important to celebrate the journey with them and not criticize their choices. Be the coach they need.

Failure to Launch: How to Get Your Teens and Young Adults to Independence

Now you have the list of career interests as well as lists of strengths and weaknesses. You want them to start and research one or maybe two of those areas of interest. One can be the predominate field of employment and education and the other a hobby. Adam works in the clothing business but he does think of getting his pilot's license because he enjoys flying. You want exposure to the fields and to get them to look for information around these professions. They want to know what sorts of jobs are in the fields, what sorts of jobs appeal to them. For example, Adam would probably do very well selling planes or teaching classes. Yet my other friend, Kelly, has a son, Patrick, who is full of adventure and energy. Patrick loves mountain biking and rock climbing, and took flying lessons on his own in high school with money he earned from working. He loves the flying and wants to be a pilot. He also is mechanical and might be able to be an airplane mechanic. Same field, different jobs to fit different personalities. We must teach our young adults to figure out how to look for opportunities in fields where they will find some satisfaction. Life is long. My father was very mechanical and might have done better being a mechanic. He had been one in the Air Force in WWII, but he could only rut think. Get a job to support the family and the car factories were hiring. He never had the Internet or even the belief that he could go and inquire about being an airplane mechanic. We need to participate and help our young adult do that sort of research. Hands on research can be intimidating when you are a young person. Heck, it has been daunting for me as an adult and I'm pretty assertive. You have to be willing to ask questions when you might not look too bright. Practice reduces the intimidation as you develop the skill set. I have also found that when it is your child you are doing it for, it is much easier for you than it is for them. Here again, we can become a team and do it together. This is a great chance to create a game plan between you and your young adult as to who is going to research what aspect of the field. I have taken Richard to investment seminars and I will ask the questions he leans over to ask me. It becomes a great adventure together. It gives us something to talk about. Adam took pilot ground school lessons on his own, but I found that when Richard wanted to take classes he seemed intimidated. I suggested that we both take the lessons. I could see myself being a pilot as a hobby. Our teacher commented to me in an e-mail that he thought that was awesome. He said he wished his mom had taken lessons with him as a teen because it would have given them something to talk about. I really want to see more parents relating to their teens and young adults as people who share interests and care about each other. Authoritarian parenting or being Helicopter parents deprives us of having powerful, loving relationships with our children. We need to be partners in their lives; it can't be our way only.

My cousin, Thomas, who is so critical of his son, shot down his son's desire to attend an art school outside the state in Iowa. Thomas immediately decided it was too expensive (not that he inquired) and criticized his son's "money grows on trees" attitude in suggesting such a place. What could he have done to promote the process? He could have asked his son what sorts of art fields interested Alex. Was Alex interested in commercial work in the animation industry? Would he like to do computer graphics, or maybe architecture? This was a great opportunity to start exploring who Alex is and what gifts and talents he can bring to this world and to create his life. Look for opportunities to take field trips together or road trips together to explore your children's interests. I know of parents who try to get their teens and young adults to go on trips that interest the parent but those days when kids tagged along are over. Thomas knew nothing of art as far as I know, and I suspect that was part of the discouragement. Alex became a young man retreating into a world of

122

Chapter 12 If Not College, Then What?

silence and sullen disappointment. After all, if we don't believe in them and their dreams, who does? You have to see your teens or young adults as gemstones in the rough. Are they diamonds, rubies, or emeralds? It takes some polishing and real interest to find out.

If you have had some of these conversations then you are researching their hopes and dreams and getting some ideas of majors in college if that is where they plan to go. Remember our old friends, plan B and plan C? I talk to so many parents who think only of one option: College. It you have them on the road of what they can begin to learn about in college, great! But keep open the idea that maybe they also need to work in the field. Work is for money or experience. You cannot buy experience. It too is valuable. Get them into the field working in some capacity. Perhaps at one point they may need to drop out and work for a while. Be open to the idea of how to advance their resume while going to college. Be flexible that they may need to take some time to work in the field. Once I counsel people that there is no shame if their young adult isn't ready for a straight four years of college after high school so they need to prepare for the work world, they seem relieved. Our parent peers are all bragging about their college bound young adults. If you have a young adult on the road to independence, you can brag too. In fact, you should be really proud. Even the parents with college bound students are hoping one day (like on graduation), they too will have independent young adults making good money when the statistics say that is not likely to happen. Be proud of whatever your teen or young adult is doing to move to adulthood. They've earned it and so have you!

I put myself through my first year of college. I found the grants and scholarships to pay for it. My mother made it very clear that in our working class family, if there was any money for college, it would go to the boys who in that day and age would have to be the bread winners of the family. Girls were just going to get married and have babies; college was a waste except to make a good match and good marriage. I dropped out the second year, overwhelmed with coming up with the financial backing and living on my own. I had a job in the hospital working as a nurse's aide the first summer following my first year in college. I worked at that for a while and then decided to work in an upscale and busy boutique. My mother had been a very successful Avon lady and before her marriage had worked her way up to being a buyer in a successful department store. Maybe I had inherited some of those genes. It only took two months before I realized I did not like working in clothing retail. None of it fulfilled me like helping people get well and go back to their lives. There was more of real life and drama than you ever see on the TV shows. I had to learn things about myself in that regard. I went back to the hospital and back to college part-time because I missed the intellectual stimulation. Sometimes we need to find out about ourselves to move forward successfully. I hear stories like this all the time from parents. We need to trust our young adults are finding their way to careers and good jobs. It is done so much easier with supportive parenting.

If plan B is to find a way to work in the chosen field part-time or by internship and maybe take some time to work in it full-time, plan C should be looking to see if maybe there is a better route to becoming what we want to be through trade or technical schools. Some degrees like this can be done online and some offer 18-month programs for students who come out certified in their field and with an Associate's degree. Most also have job placement that is as high as 90-95 percent in the chosen field. You will not find those statistics in colleges. Look at all the roads your student can go down and don't get overly attached to any of them. Timelines for achievement have to be flexible. In all of this the student should be learning life skills of managing money, time, and how to deal with people as real adults. Sometimes the picture is cluttered further by romances. A lot is going on in these early adult years and don't forget that their brains are still developing.

All right, you have found out some interests, strengths, and ways to work in the field. These are the first two years of college if your student is going that route or the early years in the work force or job training. If they are in college some colleges require that you declare a major upon entering and tailor general education classes throughout and in consideration of those majors. In others, they don't let you declare majors until your third year. By the summer after the second year, it is critical that your young adult is working in that field or in a related field. Do not waste summer jobs on bagging groceries. The young adult needs to be lining up possible employment by getting job connections. In all of this, you are there to support and check out how they are seeing the journey. You are not there to direct the journey. Assist through research and connections of your own. Help them verbalize what they see as the game plan. Justin has a stepbrother, Brad, who went to Princeton on a football scholarship. He was clearly a bright young man. He got his degree in history. He finished and came home to live with mom. Did anyone ever ask him how he saw that degree translating into a career? Never once did he spend a summer or any time in an internship or job that he could transit into. A high school counselor told me once that she doesn't like sending students into the technical schools because they cost so much and she hates to see them have expensive loans to pay back after the 18 months. As I said, with most having job placement, how is that worse than someone coming home from college with student loans over four years or investments by parents for four years only to have them qualified to work in fast food? More and more stories are coming out about young adults graduating college into their first job at $33,000 only to find out how difficult it is to live on and pay back student loans. One story recounted to me of a student was that it was probable with his student loans and credit card debt, he would be free of the obligations in his 40's. That is not what we parents want for our children. With that kind of burden, forget a family and a house. These young adults don't understand the impact of credit or credit scores and what their financial activity in college is doing to their lives in the long term.

Brad was never asked, to my knowledge, about his career interests or assisted in finding work in his fields of interest. This is sadly the case with most parents. They don't dialogue or help their young adult figure out a game plan for a job. "College is not a job" is a very true quote I once heard. Make use of your connections. Help land your young adult or your teen a job. They don't know how to do it. That really is your job. Some parents have and will disagree with me, but remember, young adults still have the child brain and the child brain is still looking for model adult behavior. If you don't put out that expectation and find the models, you are only enabling them to remain children. Isn't that the problem here? We want them to "grow up". This is our job. And the good news is that it creates a new adult-to-adult relationship with them. Many parents are afraid of not being needed or wanted in their young adult's lives. That won't happen if you are their biggest fan and support.

Chapter 12 If Not College, Then What?

Now they are off to college with majors in mind, ideas of where they are going, what they want to check out. You have a game plan and that graduation date with the degree, and the job connections are looking good and then they drop out of school. Now what?

Jobs and Technical Schools

I have seen this happen at several junctures. Maybe it happens right after leaving high school. All the talk of college may inspire some students to keep up with their peers and opt for the community college or junior college route initially, but then after the first semester they may drop out. I keep encouraging parents to think in terms of options because they will be better prepared whenever this happens. Some students make it through the first year. I have seen other students who have gone to a college they don't really find is a good fit once they are there. Colleges generally discourage transfer until the students have completed the initial two years, but my oldest transferred to a local community college near the college he wanted to get into and found his second year more rewarding at the community college level. Transfers aren't that hard. Some students think they must go through the same application and testing process they went through applying from high school. This isn't true. But sometimes students drop out after the two years of general education or two years at a community college. Parents need to be keeping their eyes and ears open for work opportunities or career college options. What you want is to get your child into some system that will let them work. If you have been giving your teen or young adult responsibilities and skill sets all along, once they hit the work world, they are generally ready to go off and be independent.

I know several young people finishing their undergraduate degrees and they are putting off graduate school. This happens too. Either they want a breather after years of grueling homework and class routines or they didn't make it into the graduate programs they applied to and want a year or two to recoup. The parents generally like the idea of their child returning home but this gets to be problem for most. Even if the young adult is working, parents are looking for companionship that was similar to when the students were in high school. At this point, the young adults have had enough freedom that they don't care for the house rules anymore. They see their parents more like roommates and want the same adult respect. Be prepared to start looking for housing with them. Sometimes it does work out. I've known a mother who let her daughter and boyfriend move back for the summer. Everyone got along great but by and large the complaining and irritation starts when the parents realize that maybe the young adult wants cooked meals and laundry done like the old days but doesn't want to share in household chores. Both sides have moved into new roles but remnants of old ones remain and the fear of not being respected becomes the elephant in the room on both sides.

I frequently counsel parents and say if the young adult is moving home, you need a game plan. There has to be a time-line. If it's for the summer in between school years then that is easy. But other vague goals such as "until he gets on his feet" are not a time-line. When Justin moved in, we agreed to six months with the proviso that we would re-evaluate the situation as benchmarks were or were not made. Six months is generally a good starter. First off is to get a full time job or two part-time jobs. Make

125

sure they have their driver's license as being without it limits their job and living situation choices. It is good to have them pay rent and other household fees to cover some water, electricity, and food choices. Lastly it is good to start looking at living situations, seeing what the cost of situations are. This also lets them know that the situation is temporary and gets them to think of what they want and how they can afford it.

You don't do them any favors by letting them spend long times at home unemployed or underemployed. They need to experience life with all of its problems. That is how they discover mastery of situations. It builds up their self-confidence and it is good for you to begin to have some time for you. They will make mistakes. It is how they resolve them that gives the measure of the person. Learn to be comfortable with them being responsible and encourage it. It is good for both of you.

Career college as a career path never really gets discussed with the majority of students in high school. They are either not told how to figure out entering the work world unless they are in the Career Tech Programs or they are encouraged to go to community/junior colleges or four year colleges. Career Tech Programs tend to be for only a small number of students. They work in conjunction with business partners in the community that need a new work force to replace a large retiring population, the Baby Boomer generation. We need a skilled work force and yet high schools do not address this need. Education remains very estranged from real world skills. The very curriculum of high schools is designed to meet the requirements of colleges who likewise are fairly estranged from real world jobs and careers. Yet when teens and young people go through hands on programs learning real work force skills, the behavior problems experienced by most teachers go out the window. I have never seen more involved and more passionate teachers than I have seen in the Career Tech Program. The students appreciate and care about these teachers, which is not typical with so many other average classrooms and teachers. These teachers want to see their students succeed and when career tech students get to see themselves with work skills in work situations, they feel more confident being treated by adults as adults. With a third of our high school students dropping out and statistics showing that the majority of students entering college are women, we need to make education more relevant and more concrete for our teens and young adults and especially young men. As education stands now in the high school and university realms, it is too esoteric and too academic without the touches of a real world basis. "Soft skills" are another thing being taught in these Career Tech programs. Soft skills are the ones that teach young people how to act and interact. Young people need to learn how to be professional in dealing with others, whether it is customers or fellow workers. They learn how to interview for jobs and write resumes and cover letters. I was interviewed once for my coaching expertise and I explained that by and large, college graduates are unprepared for the job-hunting process. The interviewer was stunned. He was sure that they have been taught these skills. We have English requirements that go on forever it seems, but they seldom address real world English use. This would be a good place to teach soft skills but English remains a largely outmoded requirement with little relevance to life. All of these skills get addressed in Career Tech Programs and in Career colleges. In both of these there is a partnership for promoting the candidate into the job force and job recruiters know that these are the places to find trained young people. These two models should be adopted by our high schools and colleges. Parents assume they are present there when they are not.

Chapter 12 If Not College, Then What?

Since they are not present in our high schools and colleges, it is the parent who needs to help the teen and young adult achieve them. This brings me to the choices we are making for the world of academics only. Students are encouraged to take high-level courses commonly called AP (Advanced Placement) such as AP English or AS (Advanced Standing) such as AS History. These classes indicate more rigorous work and often have hours of homework. With testing, students can place out of college classes and it looks good on the college application. Testing is all that seems to be on the mind of parents and schools. No test is definitive, so more come along trying to discern an easy way to evaluate and classify your child. In California, we have an exit test from high school that students have to take to get their diploma. Even though students have been passed in classes, the stories have been that students graduated without the basic skills in reading and writing. This is to make sure they leave school with these basics. Aside from all the tests coming out for college entrance such as the SAT (Scholastic Assessment Test) and the ACT (American College Testing Program), we in California have STAR testing (Standardized Testing and Reporting) which takes place over a number of days. The problem with testing is that it says pretty much nothing except how well the student can figure and perform that test. The theory is that it is measuring something. Whether it is intelligence, the work product of the teacher teaching the curriculum, or the ability of the student to learn from the teacher, we continue the testing hoping for some clarity. But we do know it isn't measuring any of these things so as to justify their expense and time consumption. We just don't have any other tool. Most parents are never told they can exempt their students from these standardized tests given in the public schools. You can and you should. I wrote a simple letter every year denying my permission for them to test my child. It is time we stopped all this testing.

I have attended school board meetings where the principals of the schools come to explain why their school didn't perform as well as hoped. There are tons of factors involved in evaluating a school like this. Public schools have to take everyone and in some with lower socio-economic populations, education is a low priority and a low value. The list goes on and on and my heart breaks for teachers and principals trying to do a good job while being evaluated by this one measure of performance. I noticed early on in elementary school that not only were the days of long, stressful testing affecting my sons, but the test itself was causing undue anxiety as well. Teachers pressured by administrators were pressuring students to do well. The test also had questions above the grade level of the students to try and catch the genius students or teachers who got better performance out of their students. For the kids this often meant they would get a question they hadn't a clue about and self-doubt would set in. Had they not paid attention in class? Were they just so dumb that they not only didn't learn it, they couldn't remember it to begin with? When I saw the stress this was generating on my little children, I withdrew my permission for them to be tested. In every single school, I got called and attempts were made to bully me because this too would reflect badly on the school and they would risk losing monetary rewards. Secretly teachers applauded me because they were sick and tired of teaching for a test. When I tell parents that the children don't have to take the tests, they are shocked. They don't know they have that right, and I warn them, they will be bullied or guilt induced to change their minds if they decline to have their children tested. You need to stand up for your child.

Failure to Launch: How to Get Your Teens and Young Adults to Independence

I will never forget how the vice principal in the high school called me up, angry with me. How could I cause damage to his school like this? I told him a number of kids simply blow off the test, answering randomly or not taking it seriously. Why are schools subjecting these young people to days of testing? That is brutal! I took the California Bar Exam to become an attorney and that is three full days of testing. It is emotionally wrenching for an adult and yet we do a similar thing to young kids? Is there no concern for the children? When I told him I noticed the test was producing test anxiety in my sons and their welfare came first, he dismissed that with more comments about what I was doing to his school. I said we'd have to agree to disagree. For me, my child's welfare comes first and for him it is his school. He was not happy.

It was a little better for my sons. As I told friends, this was a lesson in civil disobedience. In lower grades they either got to sleep in and join their classmates when the test was over for the day or they went to school and studied in the library or a classroom. Even in middle school, the counselor took the small group of students not taking the test down the hill for a smoothie at Jamba Juice. By high school, snippy office people had no good plan, and my sons wound up in a study hall. When I told one parent about the experience, she commented she wish she knew parents could refuse as her son also suffered from test anxiety and didn't do well. We still need to protect our students from the relentless test evaluation that drives schools. With their egos damaged by all this evaluation is it any wonder they lack self-esteem or resort to drugs, alcohol, and sex? My youngest son is like me; he is academically inclined. But for my older son, school is dull unless it relates to the real world in a meaningful way. These students need to develop a better work resume. That is the other half of the puzzle and the one we neglect. I urge parents to get their teens and young adults working. This may be the very area that they will shine in and take off in. That may mean that the focus on academics needs to be toned down. It is not a bad thing or the end of the world. Remember, the whole goal is to get a good job and a good career and another way to come at that is through work and volunteer experiences. In fact, that is the stronger way to come at it. We need to take back the lives of our children so that they are developing more normally in these years. It also strengthens your bonds with your teen or young adult if they see you come to their defense from the onslaught of school administrators. It is a mistake to assume that administrators are interested in our students' welfare. If as in the Career Tech program, the students feel good about themselves and their hopes and dreams, you have a good teacher and good school, but if they feel crushed down and not so good about who they are based on their academics, you have a bad school and bad teachers. The end product shouldn't be a skilled test taker but rather a fine young adult, emerging to give back to the family and community. ♋

Conclusion

If you have a young adult still at home, you made a mistake. You thought that education alone would provide them with the life and job skills they needed to get out on their own. You are in good company. This was and is the message that our society has been given for decades. Most likely you didn't give your teen or young adult enough responsibility and freedom to make adult mistakes in order to start learning life skills. The good news is this can be corrected fairly quickly. The bad news and good news is that it means you have to change some of your parenting dynamics. In short, you are the answer.

On the one hand you have to adjust your expectations that they can make adult choices without mistakes. Their brains still resemble a child's but they must have adult experiences to start evolving. You must model good adult behavior on how to handle the world and the experiences coming your way. It is critical to mentor them through this phase. In the words of Dale Carnegie, "Don't criticize, complain, or condemn." If you can find grace and humor through the whole thing, so much the better. Make these teen and young adult years memorable in a good way not a bad way.

You have an opportunity to sit down and create a game plan for independence. This is also a chance to let your son or daughter know, maybe for the first time, that you believe in them. Believe even though you aren't sure. The power of that will take both of you far. Don't we all want someone to believe in us? Please don't be afraid to hand hold them through some of the challenges. These are great opportunities to bond. No one likes to be inept. And above all, remember you are either raising dependent adults that suck you and rest of the world dry with their needs and demands or independent adults who reflect well on your family and the job you did.

Failure to Launch: How to Get Your Teens and Young Adults to Independence

Resources

Adams, Jane. *When Our Grown Kids Disappoint Us: Letting Go of Their Problems, Loving then Anyway, and Getting on with Our Lives.* New York: Free Press, 2003.

Brott, Armin. *Father for Life: A Journey of Joy, Challenge, and Change.* New York: Abbeville, 2003.

Campbell, Ross and Gary Chapman. *Parenting Your Adult Child: How you can help them achieve their full potential.* Chicago: Northfield, 1999.

Carnegie, Dale. *How to Win Friends & Influence People.* New York: Simon & Schuster, 1988.

Clark, Chap. *Hurt: Inside the World of Today's Teenagers.* Grand Rapids: Baker Academic, 2005.

Cline, Foster and Jim Fay. *Parenting Teens with Love & Logic: Preparing Adolescents for Responsible Adulthood.* Colorado Springs: Pinon Press, 1992.

Fay, Jim. *Helicopters, Drill Sergeants, and Consultants: Parenting Styles and the Messages They Send.* Colorado: Love and Logic, 1994.

Gawain, Shakti. *The Creative Visualization Workbook: Use the Power of Your Imagination to Create What you Want in Your Life.* Rev. ed. Novato: New World Library, 1995.

Kiyosaki, Robert and Sharon Lechter. *Rich Dad, Poor Dad: What the Rich Teach their Kids About Money—That the Poor and Middle Class Do Not!* New York: Warner Books, 2000.

Lawlis, Frank. *The ADD Answer: How To Help Your Child Now.* New York: Viking, 2004.

Lawlis, Frank. *Mending the Broken Bond: The 90 Answer to Developing a Loving Relationship with Your Child.* New York: Viking, 2007.

Levine, Mel. *Ready or Not, Here Life Comes.* New York: Simon and Schuster, 2005.

McGraw, Phil. *Family First: Your Step-by-Step Plan for Creating a Phenomenal Family.* New York: Free Press, 2004.

McGraw, Phil. *Life Strategies: Doing What Works, Doing What Matters.* New York: Hyperion, 1999.

McGraw, Phil. *Self Matters: Creating Your Life from the Inside Out.* New York: Free Press, 2001.

Silverstein, Olga, and Beth Rashbaum. *The Courage to Raise Good Men: You Don't Have to Sever the Bond with Your Son to Help Him Become a Man.* New York: Penguin, 1994.

Tannen, Deborah. *You're Wearing That? Understanding Mothers and Daughters in Conversation.* New York: Random House, 2006.

Fenwick, Elizabeth and Tony Smith. *Adolescence: The Survival Guide for Parents and Teenagers.* New York: DK Publishing, 1996.

Books Related to Job Hunting

Asher, Donald. *How to Get Any Job with Any Major.* Berkeley: Ten Speed, 2004.

Bolles, Richard. *What Color Is Your Parachute? A Practical Manual for Job-Hunters and Career-Changers.* Berkeley: Ten Speed, 2008.

Farr, Michael. *300 Best Jobs Without a Four-Year Degree.* Indianapolis: JIST, 2006.

Haft, Timothy. *Trashproof Resumes: Your Guide to Cracking the Job Market.* New York: Random House, 1995.

Muhammad, Dionne. *Byond the Red Carpet: Keys to Becoming a Successful Personal Assistant.* Bloomington, Ind: AuthorHouse, 2004.

Nemko, Marty and Paul and Sarah Edwards. *Cool Careers for Dummies.* 2nd ed. Hoboken: Wiley, 2001.

Rath, Tom. *Strength Finders 2.0.* New York, Gallup, 2007.

Ryan, Robin. *60 Seconds & You're Hired.* New York: Penguin, 2000.

Yate, Martin. *Cover Letters that Knock 'Em Dead.* Holbrook: Adams Media, 1998.

Articles

Abel, Olivia and Jennifer Wren. "Home Boys: Family Chores and the Simple Life." *People Magazine* 27 March 2006: 117-122.

Grossman, Lev. "Growing Up? Not So Fast." *Time Magazine* 24 Jan. 2005: 42-53.

Nevius, C. W. "Secure in the Nest." San Francisco Chronicle Magazine 23 July 2006: 12-15.

Websites

http://www.kidsoutnow.com
For those of you looking for more help or coaching, this is my website.

http://www.anthonyrobbins.com
This is the official website of Anthony Robbins from which you can purchase books, CDs, and find seminars to attend.

Failure to Launch: How to Get Your Teens and Young Adults to Independence

http://cesarmillaninc.com
Separate from his TV show, this is the site of Cesar Millan, the Dog Whisperer, where you can buy his books, DVDs, and get coaching advice for your dog. He is an excellent source for learning how to be a calm, assertive leader of your "pack" and in your home.

http://channel.nationalgeographic.com/series/dog-whisperer
Here you will find news about the show, The Dog Whisperer, and can read blogs by Cesar Millan.

http://drphil.com
This is Dr. Phil's official website where you can buy products and find shows of interest. Although I feel he has a tendency to blame young adults living at home for their failure to master independence, he has a lot of common sense advice in many areas.

http://franklawlis.com
Dr. Lawlis sits on the advisory board of The Dr. Phil Show. He has excellent books on A.D.D., stress management, and learning disabilities which are extra challenges in launching your teen or young adult successfully.

http://supernanny.com
All that you need to know about the show, Super Nanny, is in this website. Again, like the The Dog Whisperer, this provides good role modeling for calm, assertive parenting.

http://jofrost.com
Jo Frost is the super nanny of the show with the same name. She does an excellent job connecting with teens and parents as well as with young children.

http://loveandlogic.com
I have referred numerous times to Jim Fay's parenting styles of Helicopter, Drill Sergeant, and Consultant. The Love and Logic Institute that promotes this philosophy can be found at this website.